THE ULTIMATE
BIG BARBEL
EXPERIENCE

By

Steve Stayner

A STAYNER/HARRISON PRODUCTION

Written, internally compiled and edited by Steve Stayner.

Cover photography by Steve Stayner and Steve Withers.

Cover designs and layout by Steve Stayner.

Final cover artwork and graphic design by Mark Straker.

First published in 2001 by Harrison Advanced Rods, 201 Summers road, Brunswick Business Park, Liverpool. L3 4BL.

First printed in Great Britain by Derbyshire Colour Services Ltd. Unit 6B Monk road Industrial Estate, Alfreton, Derbyshire. DE55 7RL.

ISBN 0 9540401 0 4

© Steve Stayner 2001

All rights reserved. No part of this publication may be reproduced or transmitted in any form or by any means, electronic or mechanical, including photocopy, recording, or any information storage and retrieval system; without permission in writing from the author.

AUTHOR'S ACKNOWLEDGEMENTS

Special thanks go to Chris Newbold for his time and close-up SLR photography: to Brian and Joy Dowling, Alex Young, Bill Paxman, Howard Maddocks, Dave Currell, Steve Pope, Tim Jacklin, Alan Henshaw, Nick Eyre and Steve Withers for all of their help, photographic support and words of encouragement. My very special thanks go to my mother, Ruby, and father, George Stayner. And, to Dr Steve Harrison, without the support of whom this book may not have been published.

CONTENTS

FORWORD 6-7
By Dr Steve Harrison

CHAPTER 1

A WORD FROM THE AUTHOR 8
THE MAGNIFICENT BARBEL 8-9
BIG BARBEL BEHAVIOUR 10
WHEN IS A BARBEL BIG? 10-11
LOCATION 11-13

CHAPTER 2 TACKLE

INTRODUCTION 14-15
MAINLINE AND HOOKLENGTH MATERIALS 15-19
HOOK PATTERNS 19-22
KNOTS 22-23
SWIVELS 24
WEIGHTS 24-25
THERMOMETER 25-26
POLARISED SUNGLASSES 26
WHICH REEL? 26-27
RODS 27-29
A GUIDE TO ROD BUILDING 29-41

CHAPTER 3 BAITS

INTRODUCTION 42-43
MAGGOTS AND CASTERS 43-44
CORN 44
MEAT 44-45
HEMP 45
CHEESE 45-46

WORMS 47-48
MINNOWS 48
MEALWORMS 48-49
DESIGNER BASE MIXES 49-50
FLAVOURINGS AND ADDITIVES 50-55
THE ULTIMATE DESIGNER 56-57

CHAPTER 4 TACTICTS (SUMMER)

TWO RODS: ONE HOOK 59
SIGHT SELECTION 59-61
CHOPPED MAGGOTS AND CASTERS 61-62
TOUCH LEGERING 63-64
FLAVOURING AND FREEZING MAGGOTS 64
GASSED MAGGOTS 64-65
THE BIG-BAIT METHOD 65-67
CUTTING AND HOOKING BIG BAITS 81-82
HAIR RIGGING 83-85
HEMP BOMBS 85-87
INTO THE WILDERNESS 87-88
THE THREE-SWIM ROTATION SYSTEM 88-89
KNOT TYING 90-92
HOOKLENGTHS AND RIGS 93-98
ROUTINE MAINTENANCE 99-101
THE ULTIMATE BIG BARBEL EXPERIENCE 102-104
DEMORALISATION 104-106
RETURNING TO BASICS 106-109

(AUTUMN AND WINTER) 110

WATER TEMPERATURE 111-115
UNDER PRESSURE 116-120
BEWARE THE CRYSTAL BALL 120-121
BAIT SIZE AND QUANTITY 121
GRID FISHING 122-125
FISHING IN THE DARK 125-127

CHAPTER 5

REPRODUCTION 127-133
PHOTOGRAPHING FISH 133-140
CONCLUSION 141-142
BIG BARBEL HANDLING CODE 143-144

USEFUL ADDRESSES

MISCELLANEOUS 145
TACKLE SHOPS 146
BAITS AND TACKLE ACCESSORIES 147
BARBEL ANGLING TUITION 148

USE EASY FIND INDEX AT FOOT OF EACH PAGE.

FORWORD
By Dr Steve Harrison

It is a winding road that led to Harrison Advanced Rods getting involved in publishing this book, our first venture into the world of publishing. For the last two years, we have been focussed on our core business of making rods and blanks for the most demanding of specialist applications, and that has kept us pretty busy. Steve Stayner and I met for the first time in 1998 and have been talking about Barbel rod design ever since. Like most successful anglers, Steve is obsessive about his tackle and bait, and we helped him get the rods he needed to bank double figure Barbel on a regular basis. Gradually it emerged that Steve had been working on a manuscript for a specialist Barbel book, and because of the work we had done together on rods, he asked me to look at the draft pages on rod building and design. As a result I somehow got sucked into the project.

Since then, Steve has written a few pages for our website and we have exchanged views on many related subjects from hooks to baits, and I have been allowed to see a few more pages of this book. But overall, as a company, we have no editorial input and this book is Steve's ideas alone on how to catch more Big Barbel. That said, this venture has given me a taste for this publishing, so you can expect to see more books on specialist angling from Harrison Advanced Rods in the future.

Although chance played a big part in bringing Steve Stayner and Harrison's together, I finally decided to give our support to this project because of the quality of original ideas, and the experience of the author. Plus of course the author has been quite flattering towards our rods! However, anyone who knows Steve will tell you his support is not up for sale, and his advise has not been tainted by any sponsorship from us; or as far as we know any hook, line, reel or bait manufacturer. Most unusual in these days of professional anglers and blatant product placement!

Barbel fishing is changing. Fish are getting bigger and more widespread, but conditions are also changing, with rivers holding higher levels for longer. Maybe more significantly, the number of anglers chasing big Barbel is increasing. Barbel are getting wary of traditional techniques and baits. This book shares innovative ideas on many topics that will help give any committed angler the edge to keep them amongst the big fish.

Steve Harrison

CHAPTER 1

A WORD FROM THE AUTHOR
THE MAGNIFICENT BARBEL
BIG BARBEL BAHAVIOUR
WHEN IS A BARBEL BIG?
LOCATION

A WORD FROM THE AUTHOR

It's seventeen years since I captured my first ever Barbel, a Trent fish of around one and a half pounds. A small fish by anyone's standards, but so huge was the impact of the experience that the foundations of infatuation were laid instantly and firmly in place. Ever since that mid-July afternoon of 1984 I have been a single species angler, whose sole piscatorial pleasure is derived only by seeking to capture what must surely be the most beautiful, awe inspiring and powerful fish that swim in our inland waters.

Even to this day, my admiration for the Barbel grows and as each season progressively unfolds, my thirst for yet more knowledge and understanding of the way in which the bigger specimens behave still remains unquenchable. Such is this difference in behaviour that we must target them almost as a completely different species to that of their smaller brethren. This book outlines in detail some of the knowledge I have so far amassed. Its primary objectives being to educate, re-educate, update, inform, inspire and support those who dare to do battle with these most awesome of Barbel. **Steve Stayner**

THE MAGNIFICENT BARBEL

No other fresh-water fish possesses the power to captivate an angler's imagination more than the Barbel. Perhaps it is this very realisation which is responsible for their on-going increase in popularity, as each season we witness many anglers of different species, including carp, falling victim to the Barbels' narcotic-like allure. Add to that their overall increase in average size, population and national availability, and we could well be on the verge of a Barbel fishing epidemic.

So, just what is it about the Barbel that we all find so appealing? My own view is that if we are to fully appreciate all that the species represents to us, we must look far beyond its legendary and completely unrivalled fighting qualities to a place that exists deep within our very own imaginations. Ever since our infant years through adolescence and beyond, we have been subjected to, and enchanted by, the power of beauty and fascination, elegance and splendour, and of magic and mystique. All of these influential attributes are synonymous to the Barbel – especially, Big Barbel – and, once combined, make up the characteristics of a creature that is no less than magnificent.

Whether we are consciously aware of them or not, it is all of these endearing qualities that capture the heart of every Barbel angler; often fuelling that irresistible and uncontrollable urge to visit the wonderful environments in which they live. As the child remains forever within us all, it is little wonder that we can find the call of the Barbel so difficult to resist. So bewitched can we become, that we are all but powerlessly drawn to the river as if by some magical, invisible, almost telepathic force – driven only by the all encompassing passion that many of us feel for this most noble of species.

With all of this going on within our minds – if only subconsciously – it's not surprising that we can, at times, feel almost compelled to go fishing. Taken to the extreme, we may become so obsessively compelled that we begin to risk the very stability of the relationships that we have with our partners. If the relationship is not so good then Obsessive Compulsive Barbel Fishing Disorder (O.C.B.F.D) is arguably justified. But where it is healthy and loving we should at least try to curb our obsession and lay tribute to the "Barbel fishing widows" that we can so selfishly leave behind.

BIG BARBEL BEHAVIOUR

As their survival as a species depends upon it, mother nature dictates that all Barbel are inherently cautious creatures. However, nobody could argue against the fact that often the smaller fish of seven pounds and below can prove ridiculously easy to catch. Occasionally this can be said of the bigger specimens, but far more usually their instinctive caution is much more difficult and time consuming to overcome.

Even where they are present in a stretch of river that is extremely pressured by many a competent angler, a large fish is more than capable of evading capture for many months on end. This in no way implies that all big Barbel are clever, but there is increasing evidence which suggests that certain individuals wise up to the over-used methods/baits adopted by the angler to capture them. This "danger by association" is more applicable to the hours of daylight and clear-water conditions. And with many controlling clubs carrying bans on night fishing, the odds against their capture swing more heavily in the Barbels' favour.

WHEN IS A BARBEL BIG?

Although the contents of this book are specifically tailored to assist the reader in the successful and consistent capture of Big Barbel, the size at which we regard a fish as big is dependant upon a number of factors.

Firstly, we must take into account the potential of the venue we wish to target. By taking note of its Present River record and average size of fish, we can soon determine a realistic size of the Barbel we seek. The best example that I can give you is on a small stretch of the Great-Ouse "above Bedford." However, if we are to keep this in perspective, we must accept that the situation here is so far unique and should in no way be the yardstick by which we measure the potential of any other venue.

As we are all aware, this particular stretch is capable of producing half a dozen or more fish in excess of 19.lbs. It is also supported by a number of 'slightly smaller' back-up fish that may well secure its current status as a premier Barbel fishery for a few more years to come. And so, realistically speaking, a Barbel of 14.lbs+ from here would be a satisfactory target. However, a different venue on the same river with a smaller stamp of fish could see a 10.lbs+ specimen become a handsome proposition.

If we move up north to Yorkshire's River Swale, a 9.lbs+ specimen becomes as healthy an achievement as it does from Shropshire's middle Severn or the Derbyshire Dove. Nevertheless, it's extremely important for us to remember that there are still many areas throughout the country where a nine is as rare as a double.

LOCATION

By far the easiest, time saving and cost effective method of locating Big Barbel is to be reliably informed of exactly where they are. Big fish are becoming more accessible to almost everyone and a small annual fee gains us entry to The Barbel Society. With its current 1600+ strong membership of enthusiastic Barbel anglers, it shouldn't be too difficult for us to find out where to look. The Society also controls a number of its own syndicate waters, a few of which contain some very large fish. Payment of the appropriate additional fees should give you access to them. (See useful addresses)

The match anglers are another great source of information, especially if we can witness the weigh-in. This gives us the opportunity to chat to the angler who's been "smashed up" three times on 8.lb line by fish that he swears were massive. We aren't sure whether to believe him or not until we see the two eight's and the nine hit the scales. And it becomes even better when we consider that matches often give us the opportunity to witness an angler in every peg, consequently saving us months of hard work had we attempted the prospects of fishing the stretch blindly.

Our next option comes only through the experience of watercraft and a deep understanding of the species in general. Many of us, while capable of locating a few fish through the art of watercraft, rarely understand that finding a number of swims containing smaller Barbel doesn't necessarily mean we can find those which contain the larger fish. Through years of frequent misleading conditioning, it is often natural for us to regularly associate the species with moderate to fast flowing water. But, if we are to improve our chances of finding new and productive Big Barbel swims, we must be willing to search the slower and deeper areas contained within our venue, for it is in these that the true monsters we may seek are far more likely to be found.

One of the worst problems that we can associate with searching out potential holding areas in these slower stretches is the time it often involves to do it effectively. As the pace of the surface water rarely indicates their position, finding underwater features becomes automatically more difficult, and so any potentially productive swims will often need plumbing to find any variations within their depth. Depending upon the size of our stretch, it can take us many weeks to build up the necessary profile and confidence that is needed for us to attempt fishing it, therefore it is always good for us to frequently return to areas that we already know are productive. (See 'Into the Wilderness' and 'Return to Basics')

A typical bridge swim.

Whether the water that we are searching is of moderate pace or relatively slower, there will always remain certain types of swims that we must be prepared to search - especially when fishing blindly.

Permanent features such as concrete bridge pillars that form an obvious diversion in both current speed and flow can be of the most productive type. But a great deal of this type of swim's potential depends on both the exact position of the pillar and formation of the riverbed that surrounds it. Even when we have found a productive bridge-swim, it is not always just a simple case of casting behind the pillar once the water level increases. In some instances Barbel will vacate these areas completely during times of flood. Not necessarily because the extra water has made the swim inhospitable, but more likely because the course of the river upon which food is normally delivered has been severely diverted. Once we find exactly where it's been diverted to - and it is unlikely to be far away - we will begin to catch during any conditions.

Fallen trees often make for ideal Big Barbel swims – at least temporarily!

The same principle applies to both semi-permanent and non-permanent snags. (Semi = overhanging trees attached closely to the bank with branches and/or roots in the water. Non = trees and other large snag-forming debris already resting on the riverbed.) An increase in current speed from a rising river may also cause the fish to vacate these areas and nothing should be taken for granted. Very often, the locations of the right kind of snags in the right sort of area makes a swim for all conditions, but not always!

CHAPTER 2 TACKLE

TACKLE INTRODUCTION
MAINLINE AND HOOKLENGTH MATERIALS
HOOK PATTERNS
KNOTS
SWIVELS
WEIGHTS
THERMOMETER
POLARISED SUNGLASSES
WHICH REEL?
RODS
A GUIDE TO ROD BUILDING

TACKLE INTRODUCTION

There is no other form of fresh-water fishing in this country where the correct choice of tackle is more important than when we are Big Barbel fishing. Thankfully, the onset of the new Millennium has brought with it the refreshing signs of change towards the way in which we view the importance of strength within our set-up. And not before time!

A few years have now passed since I began to question the misguided information of the so-called experts who constantly recommended the use of completely inappropriate tackle. Although the remnants of the 'Old school' cash and fish costly advise on line strength and rod design are to a certain extent still with us, hopefully the next few years will witness their complete and total demise.

More recent years have seen the introduction of many items of tackle aimed at the specimen Barbel hunter, and as the cult-like following of the species increases, we will undoubtedly see the market become even more saturated than it already is. As we are all aware, quality specialist fishing tackle does not come cheap, but as we will see in this chapter, the very best that we require for the job doesn't always have to be the most expensive.

MAINLINE AND HOOKLENGTH MATERIALS

MONO OR BRAIDED MAINLINES?

At present there are so many braided mainlines on the market that it is difficult not to be taken in by some of the advertising jargon that accompanies them. After all, who wouldn't be quietly and confidently impressed if they were using a virtually indestructible reel line that had a wet-knot strength of 20.lbs and the diameter of the average 6.lb mono?

Once my own curiosity had got the better of me I was tempted into giving one of them a try. I quickly came to the conclusion that, had I continued to use my particular choice of dynema-based braid for more than half a dozen sessions, I may well have had a heart attack. The virtual zero stretch factor in this type of line gave me a strangely uneasy feeling that I would lose everything that I hooked. I dare not lean into a fish with the confidence that a little stretch has to offer for fear that the hook would tear out.

To counter this manufacturers tell us to set the reel clutch accordingly, but doesn't this defeat the object of not giving them any line in the snag-infested swims that these braids are so often recommended for? Where is the sense in using 20.lb line if we have to let the fish run to keep the hook in? I know that many anglers are at ease with braid as a mainline, but as far as I am concerned, it is of use for hook-lengths only!

WHICH MONOFILLAMENT?

Having established the importance of having a degree of stretch within our mainline now leaves us to make our choice from the vast array of monos that are currently available. Before we do this, however, we must first consider a number of other factors, the most important being abrasion resistance, strength to diameter, and to a certain extent, suppleness. When daytime fishing in clearer water, colour of our line must be considered, for obviously we want it to be as low in visibility as possible.

Many of the so-called fourth generation co-polymers of today offer most of these qualities, some of which have the added bonus of very high wet-knot strength. But we must consider this may be lower than stated by certain manufacturers. Another area to be wary of is the claimed abrasion resistance. Baring in mind that much of our fishing may be in the vicinity of highly abrasive snags, we are looking for the line to possess a high degree of this extremely important quality.

However, what is often overlooked about abrasion resistance is the way in which it is measured. Some manufacturers test this by repeatedly rubbing a single piece of weighted line, by pre-determined measurement, over a sharp edge. The number of oscillations that it takes for the line to wear through is what usually determines the lines abrasive qualities.

This all sounds technically acceptable until we realise that the test is done on a dry piece of line. Shouldn't it be wet? My own individual tests conclude that the addition of water to an abrasive surface makes a huge difference to these results, as certain lines which consistently gave good results when dry didn't always give such impressive results when whetted - and visa-versa.

Both its diameter and stretch factor also play an important part in a line's abrasion resistance qualities. Many monos actually stretch by an average of 35% when fully under load. Once this maximum elasticity is reached, the original pre-stretched diameter of the line is also significantly reduced, therefore making it more susceptible to wearing through to breaking point far more quickly should it come into contact with a snag.

Nevertheless, lines possessing this amount of stretch do have their advantages. Firstly, they are often quite supple and therefore offer improved presentation over stiffer materials. Secondly, they offer a greater amount of shock-absorbency against the powerful runs that a large fish can make when hooked directly under the rod top. A co-polymer that I find ideal for such situations is Fox Soft Steel. In its 10.lbs breaking strain, this line offers the perfect compromise between suppleness and high abrasion resistance.

Another more recent introduction to co-polymer technology is the excellent High Performance Carp Mono manufactured by ESP. When fishing in extremely snaggy swims I now use this line exclusively as it possesses so many of the qualities already mentioned. But, it's not until we discover this line's unrivalled wet-knot strength and abrasion resistant qualities are protected by a stretch factor of no more than 25%, that we begin to fully appreciate the true advantages of using it in these areas. If I were forced to recommend the use of only one mainline for every conceivable situation that we could possibly face it would be this one. I use it breaking strains of 10.lbs and 12.lbs and cannot praise it highly enough.

HOOK-LENGTH MATERIALS

FLUOROCARBONS

Originally designed, manufactured for and used for many years by Game-fish anglers as a tippet material, it's not until fairly recently that the hydro-invisible properties of fluorocarbons became more widely recognised by coarse and specialist anglers alike. With a specific gravity that is denser than water, this ensures any rig will sink quickly and settle tightly on the bottom, and because pure fluorocarbon also possesses the same light refractive index as water itself, once submerged it becomes invisible. Its only arguable drawback being that it is often stiff for its diameter.

At the moment, this stiffness appears variable between manufacturers; no doubt because of the huge fly angling demand for the line. However, as demand from coarse angling increases, I'm sure we will see an influx of fluorocarbons that are suppler than at present. Once this happens, we will have what is already a deadly effective product made even better. And there are encouraging signs that these improvements are happening already.

There are times however when Big Barbel hunting, where a stiff rig will be an advantage. When such a situation arises I make use of the superb Ghost manufactured by ESP. This is undeniably one of the best stiff rig materials currently available, and to be honest, I can't see that changing for quite some time.

When a suppler presentation is required, as is more often the case, I use either Grand Max Reverge in higher breaking strains, or Shakespeare Sightfree for a lighter and slightly cheaper presentation. A big drawback with pure fluorocarbons is that they can be quite expensive. Sightfree offers better value for money without compromising on quality.

Warning! Something which many of you may be tempted to do is to super-glue your knots. Never do this with fluorocarbons as the glue eats into them!

MONOFILLAMENTS

As fluorocarbons become increasingly recognised as the way forward for this type of line, it seems almost inevitable that ordinary monofillament will become less popular as a hook-length material. However, as previously mentioned, fluorocarbons are not yet the finished article and so, for the moment at least, we can still take advantage of the supple presentation that certain brands of mono can offer us.

No other mono offers a better presentation than Trilene XL, but for all that it gains us in suppleness it loses in the abrasion resistance qualities that are so common in the tougher co-polymers. We can, however, make use of XL in areas away from highly abrasive snags, such as in swims with sunken tree branches or streamer-weed etc. XL comes in weed-green or clear and is very strong for its diameter.

The co-polymer Fox Soft Steel also makes an excellent hook-length, especially when we are uncertain of what perils may lie within our chosen swim, as it offers us the 'just in case factor' of good abrasion resistance combined with a fair degree of suppleness.

BRAIDS

Used either at night or in coloured water as a complete hook-length – or as the last few inches of a fluorocarbon combi-link in gin-clear water – there's very little doubt that braids offer a more natural bait presentation and are probably accountable for the capture of more Big Barbel than any other hook-length material.

As far as the huge market for braids is concerned, it's important to remember that as Barbel anglers we need only carry a handful of different types to be fully equipped for any situation that may arise. As there are generally only two types of snag (abrasive or non-abrasive), I have now cut my own preferences to just four; all of which I carry permanently within my tackle-bag. These are 14.lb Super-silk, 15.lb Super-nova, 15.lb Snakebite and 25.lb Quicksilver. Dave Chilton's company, Kryston, manufactures all of these excellent braids.

The recommendation of using braids that are of higher breaking strain than the mainline has always been a subject for confusion and rarely understood. The reason that I use these braids is for that little extra thickness in diameter and not, as may be thought, their high breaking strain. It's also for this very same reason that I will, if circumstances demand it, increase the diameter of the mainline. I've yet to encounter a Barbel that's capable of breaking 10.lb ESP, but the extra thickness of 12, or even15.lb increases my comfort-zone when fishing near concrete.

HOOK PATTERNS

It's only as recently as a few years ago that the importation of some rather cheap and nasty foreign hooks became responsible for the lack of confidence in anything that had a chemically sharpened point. So infectious was the knock-on effect, that anglers everywhere began to inexplicably lose fish on hooks they had reliably used for years. Even today, many anglers still believe chemically etched patterns to be unreliable for snag-swim, hit and hold fishing.

While there will always be certain hooks that consistently out-perform others, I'm certain that in many cases this is down to pattern design and rarely relevant to the process by which the hook receives its point. We must also consider whether the angler is actually aware of how his or her favourite pattern is sharpened, as so many manufacturers now exclude this information from their packaging. But just because it doesn't tell us on the packet, does not mean that our totally reliable and No1 pattern is not chemically sharpened, in fact, short of a few hooks manufactured in the UK, there is every likelihood that it may have been.

If we are to be consistently successful Big Barbel anglers then there is nothing more vitally important than the point of contact. We should also be under no elusion that the very best hooks we could possibly choose to use are predominantly made in Japan. It may be sad for some people to read this, but in so many areas of engineering, including hook manufacture, the Japanese are way out in pole position.

As manufacturers endeavour to ensure we remain in contact with our fish, the last few years have brought along some radical changes to many areas within hook design. One of the most influential of these improvements as far as we Barbel anglers are concerned is the introduction of the 'stay in' beaked needlepoint. Nevertheless, it's important for us to remember that the reliability of a hook is as much dependent upon its shape as its point design.

It is also of great importance that we employ the correct pattern of hook for a specific task, as no one hook is going to be fully efficient with every method that we may need to use – at least not yet anyway! Providing that we fully understand how any one particular pattern works best, we can then reduce the necessity to carry too many different types.

For example. Only rarely while fishing near snags is it appropriate to use a hair-rig, for more often than we would prefer, we would end up hooking some immovable object on the bottom. Sometimes, however, we are fortunate enough to be able to tempt the fish out from their cover and can take full advantage of this by using the best presentation available to us.

This is without doubt the hair-rig and my favourite pattern of hook while using this method is the Kevin Nash Fang. As this hook does not possess a beaked point, the reason for its effectiveness lies totally within its shape, and because it has an inwardly turned eye, this ensures the hook spins and pricks the fish's mouth before it can eject the bait. They are awesomely reliable for presenting baits hard on the bottom. I use them in sizes 8 to 4.

Often we'll be faced with the reality of having to place our bait tight against the snag, and are left with little choice other than to forget the hair and employ the potentially less troublesome method of straight hooking.

Unfortunately, there is a likelihood that we may still frequently hook up with the bottom if we straight hook our bait and leave the point out. This leaves us with the only sensible option of burying the hook completely within the bait. However, if we are to hit bites with consistency with the point totally buried, then it follows that our hook has to be something a little bit special.

Not only must it possess the capability to tear through a large meat-bait and penetrate well into the Barbel's rubbery mouth; it must also possess the necessary tensile strength to deal with the awesome power of a large fish until it is safely landed. My favourite pattern of hook for this method is the beaked pointed T-6 Raptor manufactured by ESP. I also use this pattern for popped-up baits on a hair, for this is what the hook was originally designed for. I use them in sizes 10 to 2.

Another of my preferred patterns is the Owner SSW, model no 5111-121. I wasn't going to mention these as they always seemed extortionately expensive. However, I am pleased to hear the wonderful news that Steve Harrison is now sole distributor for Owner UK. We should now be able to obtain these superb hooks at a sensible price. I use them in sizes 8 to 2.

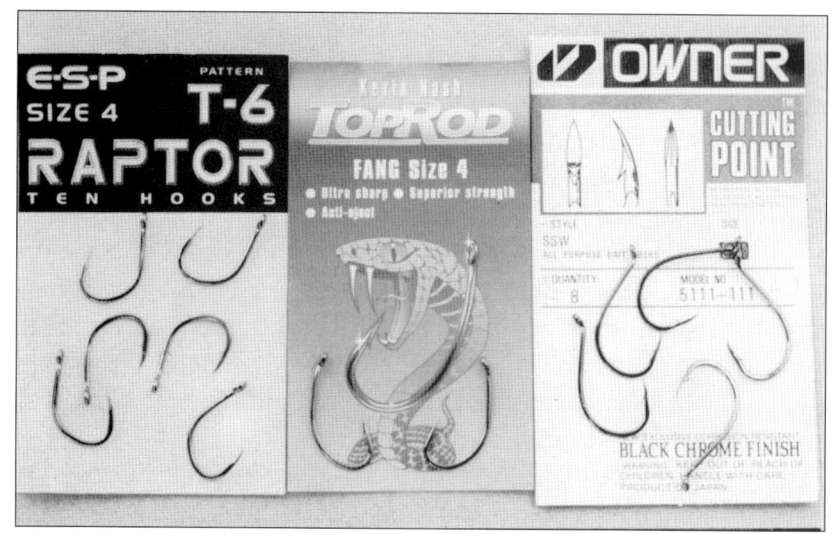

Such is the efficiency of all three chemically sharpened patterns, that they more than adequately deal with every Big Barbel situation I ask of them, consequently they all come highly recommended.

KNOTS

Whilst constructing any rig for Barbel, meticulous attention should be given to tying the all-important knots which take the strain of a hooked fish. There is absolutely no sense in us using a minimum of ten-pound line if we are tying weak knots. My own experience tells me that the 'once through the eye' blood-knot is possibly the weakest of them all. Knots of this kind need the protection of a lightly set clutch and should play no part at all in Big Barbel fishing. If you use the blood-knot, or any other knot resembling it, you will lose fish - And that is guaranteed!

The 'twice through the eye' load-bearing knots I use are, 'the knotless knot' (hook to braided hook-length when hair-rigging), 'the palomar knot' (swivel to hook-length), and 'the mahseer knot' also known as 'the trilene knot' for attaching the hook-length swivel to the mainline. All of these knots are completely reliable with the lines, hooks and swivels that I use. But, as with any other knots, they must be thoroughly checked upon tying and re-checked when hook-baits are retrieved. REMEMBER! A good knot poorly tied is equally as unreliable as bad knot properly tied. Both will result in loss of fish. Unforgivable in most circumstances! See tactics for how to tie.

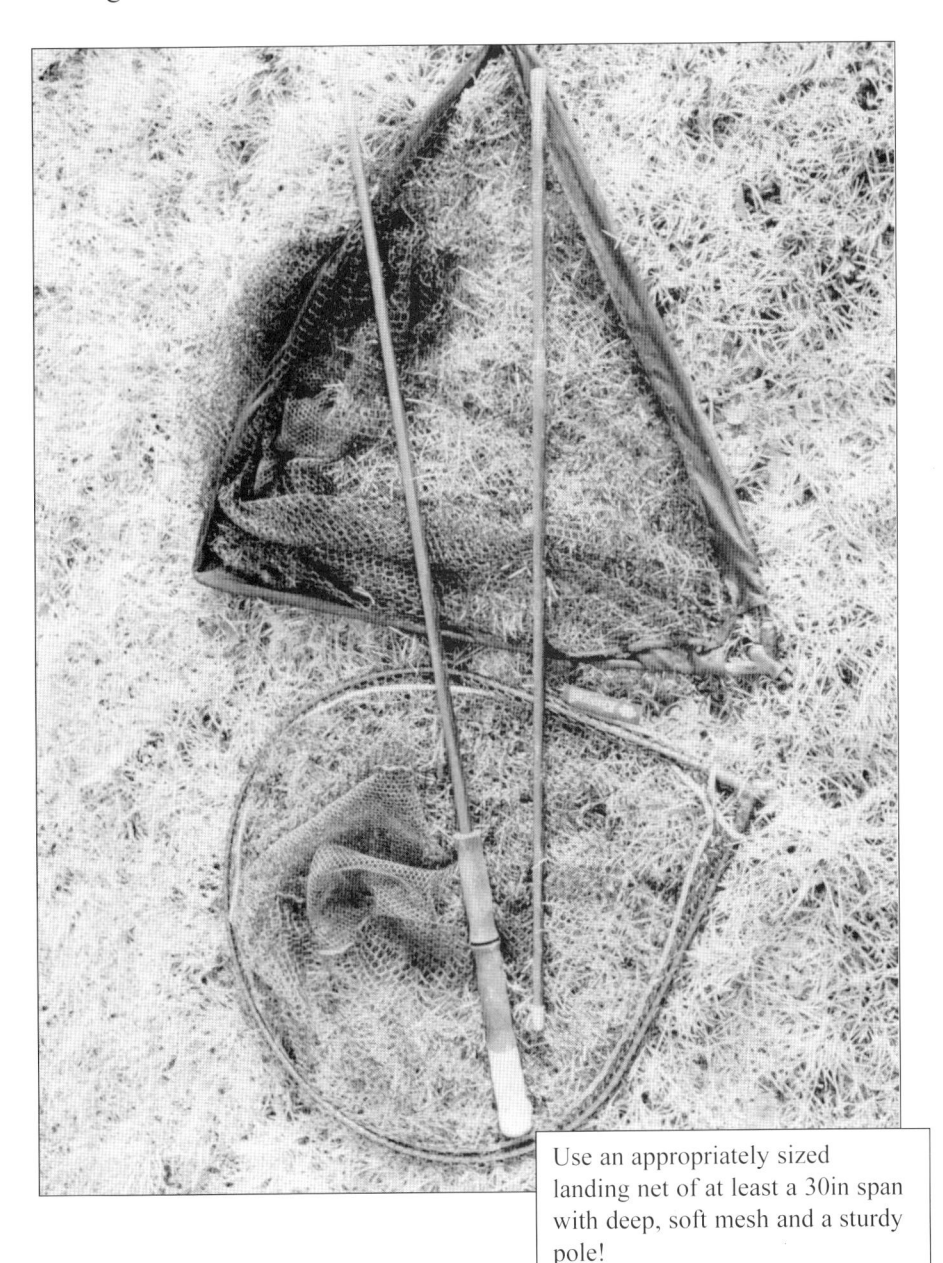

Use an appropriately sized landing net of at least a 30in span with deep, soft mesh and a sturdy pole!

SWIVELS

For every situation that I require the use of a swivel, I manage completely adequately by using only two different types in two sizes. Both are manufactured in Japan and marketed by ESP. The first is the standard 'round eye' High Performance Carp Swivel. The second is the Uni-Link Carp Swivel. I use both in sizes 9 and 10. There are a few other companies which market highly reliable swivels of both types, but it is very easy for us to pay way over the odds for some of them. ESP swivels offer an excellence in performance with a price that's very hard to beat. (See tactics for usage)

WEIGHTS

Although I make use of heavier lead weights whilst fishing wide and powerful rivers like the Trent, and in extreme flood conditions on smaller rivers, I much prefer to fish with the absolute minimum of weight required to hold bottom at any given time. This is achieved far more effectively when modelling clay is used as the anchor, as simply by adding or subtracting small amounts of material, an exact critical balance can be found.

The clay I use is of the plasticene-type, but this slightly more professional substance comes in bigger blocks and can be purchased in single colours from most good art and craft shops. I use green, light brown and black to match the bottom of my selected swim. Instead of moulding the appropriate amount of clay around a leger-stop attached to a link, as many anglers prefer, I actually mould it around a hairgrip. This reduces the cheese-wire effect that a link often produces, therefore making the whole weight more sturdy. As it can then be attached via a clip-swivel, this offers the option of quick change to a heavier lead on a rapidly rising river.

In gin-clear water, I will use a weighed pebble to match the bottom exactly. By gluing with Araldite a fluorocarbon loop to the pebble, I can then attach it to a simple running-leger rig. I mark the weight of the pebble in permanent black ink so that I instantly know the weight of each one. It's surprising how small a pebble actually holds bottom.

They sit on the contours of the riverbed perfectly and there's no way they spook the Barbel. While I certainly have no evidence to back up the theory that weights of any kind actually spook the fish, I still prefer to err on the side of caution and imagine they do. We do our prospects no harm at all when using camouflaged weights in clear-water daytime conditions.

It's always worth our while to carry both a tub of 'Drop-em' and 'Heavy metal.' These are best described as line accessories. 'Drop-em' is designed primarily to sink braided hook-links that are slightly buoyant (such as Quicksilver) and anchor them to the bottom. 'Heavy metal' is tungsten based putty-like material and can be used to add weight to hooks and trundling rigs. Dave Chilton's company, Kryston, manufactures both of these products to compliment their many hook-length materials.

Other weights that I often find useful are the Dinsmores-type flat leads from half to two and a half ounces. In high-flood conditions, I make use of the polo-shaped sea/crab leads that are around 3 to 4 ounces in weight. This is often sufficient to hold bottom when combined with a sizeable hook-bait.

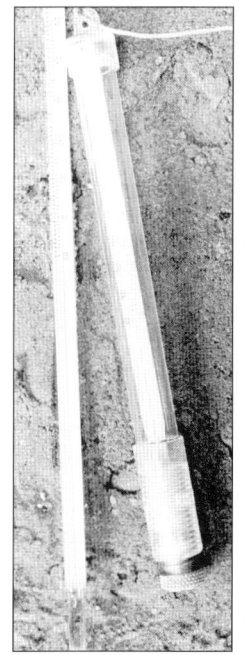

THERMOMETER

As a far clearer picture is now emerging of just how important a part any variance within water temperature can play within the roll of our success; an absolutely essential piece of equipment for us to carry throughout the autumn and winter is a thermometer. Just like many other items of tackle, thermometers can be as expensive for us to buy as we choose them to be. They even come digitally enhanced now, but this, rather surprisingly, doesn't necessarily guarantee a temperature reading of total accuracy.

While I appreciate that some of us are a little more accident-prone than others, I much prefer the older, more fragile and usually cheaper glass-type.

One in particular that I recommend is a home-brewers thermometer (pictured left.) These give a reading in both Celsius and Fahrenheit and can be purchased from most home-brewing suppliers. Try the larger outlets of Boots the Chemists.

Thermometers are also becoming more widely available through many of the larger tackle outlets nowadays. Brand names such as Rueben Heaton (pictured right), and Hardy are always looked upon with high regard. It is of course well worth remembering that both Heaton and Hardy thermometers are manufactured for anglers, and will be far less fragile than the brewers' type.

POLARISED SUNGLASSES

Another essential part of our full armoury is a good pair of polarised sunglasses. These greatly reduce the glare of reflected daylight from the surface of the water and therefore assist us in the art of fish spotting.

It's once again down to individual choice how much we would like to pay for these, as they can undoubtedly be very expensive. While some of these more expensive brands offer virtually indestructible frames with scratch-resistant lenses, I still prefer to buy a less expensive pair whenever the need arises. Before shelling out what could be a small fortune, I certainly recommend that you check out the stock within your local Boots the Chemists outlet. Their own particular brand is suitably adequate and treated with a little respect may well last a few seasons.

WHICH REEL?

Baring in mind that the majority of tactics outlined in this book are a form of static-bait legering, it shouldn't prove too difficult for us to decide on our choice of reel. All we need to be fully aware of is that a smooth clutch mechanism could either make or break our chances of landing whatever we hook. Reliability, durability and practicality are also of major importance if the reel is to serve us for many a season to come.

From purely a one reel for the job point of view, I find the Shimano 5000 GTE bait-runner to be ideal. This reel is extremely versatile and offers the option to engage the free-spool mechanism at the flick of a switch. Although – for obvious reasons – I prefer not use this facility while snag-swim fishing, in more open water the free-spool aids presentation by offering less resistance to a biting fish and is particularly useful when hair-rigging.

The Japanese engineering ensures dogged reliability, and the all-important smooth clutch and precision rear drag make playing large Barbel an absolute joy. The 5000 GTE comes with a double handle, 4 ball bearings and two spools. There's also a cheaper RE version that comes with a single handle, one spool and two ball bearings, and to be perfectly honest there isn't that much to choose between them performance wise.

These are the updated versions of the 5010 GT and Aero models. At the time of writing there are still some of these to be found in the shops and there are some great deals to be had should you be fortunate enough to find any. Something that may be of interest to the angler who occasionally prefers to touch-leger is that the older 5010's are lighter in weight than the updates. This, as well as the inevitable higher price tag of the newer versions, may well encourage you to shop around or even consider buying second hand.

RODS

It's easy to get totally carried away with the task of choosing what is arguably the most important item of tackle we are likely to buy. As it is also likely to be the most expensive, then it's important that we get it right to begin with. To help us make a wise and long-term economical choice, we must take heed of the minefield for potential miss-recommendation that is likely to both confuse and hinder our final decision.

Do we listen to the experts who recommend the use of a 1Lb 4-oz test-curve rod that in reality is more ideally suited to the likes of chub? Alternatively, do we listen to those who recommend we go to the opposite extreme by employing a 3Lb TC distance carp rod with a stiff 'poker-like' action?

Would we prefer to believe those tackle shop assistants who inform us that for our total Barbel fishing armoury to be complete, we will need a whole host of rods for every conceivable situation we are likely to encounter? According to these guys we need one for snag fishing, another for low water, one for high water, another for this method, one for that method – and so it goes expensively on!

I believe that the ideal snag-swim rod should possess an equal capacity for fish playing enjoyment no matter where we use it – whether the water is bank high or at normal level. To ensure that we are always fishing with optimum efficiency, we must refrain from entering any Big Barbel swim with a rod that is either, over, or undergunned. At the moment there is too much emphasis put upon a rod's test-curve, when the real importance regarding its performance lies within its action. For example. The current trend for what is presently regarded as the ideal test-curve and design was set many years ago. And almost as if by sheer reluctance to progress, many of us seem unable to let go of this tradition by hanging on to the 1Lb 4 oz TC all through action label.

In hit and hold snag-swim situations, we need to stop the Barbel from building up momentum and are looking for the rod to absorb the pressure in a powerful, yet deceptively subtle way. Therefore we can dispense with any idea of using a rod with a stiff unyielding action, or the far too forgiving 1.Lb. 4 oz test curve, in favour of something built totally for the task in hand.

Many Barbel rods on today's market are actually built on blanks originally designed for medium to close range carp fishing. However, anglers are becoming increasingly aware that Barbel not only fight harder (pound for pound) than carp, they also fight differently. This suggests the ideal rod would in fact be one that is specifically designed for Big Barbel. For this to be done satisfactorily and without compromise, then subtle changes to existing carp-blank patterns are probably best avoided in favour of a totally new approach with brand new ideas being put into practice.

A company already producing a range of specialist rods in exactly this way is Harrison Advanced Rods. This is an indication that Dr

Steve Harrison is now taking the Barbel rod market more seriously than ever before, and this can only be great news for those of us who fish for them.

During the introduction to this chapter, you will have read my view that the very best tackle we require doesn't always have to be the most expensive. At no other point in this book will those words emphasise that fact more than they do here because, believe me: this company leads the others just follow! While these rods are by no means the most expensive available, neither are they the cheapest. But, without a shadow of a doubt, you will not buy a better rod for the job from anywhere – no matter how much you pay for it!

The current Harrison range includes a 12-ft three-piece rod called the Tryptych, and the 'two in one' 11 or 12-ft four-piece Quorum (which can be used at either length by attaching our choice of the two different butt-sections supplied). There is also a two-piece version of the Tryptych with an identical action.

All of these rods possess the necessary progressive through actions that are ideally suited to all forms of Big Barbel fishing. Our choice depends entirely upon the length of rod we prefer. The recently released 10-ft Stalker also comes highly recommended.

A GUIDE TO RODBUILDING

While many anglers are often inquisitive of the way in which a finished rod is manufactured, most of us unfortunately remain ignorant of the whole process purely through the lack of readily available information.

I find this particular subject so fascinating that I have dedicated this segment of the book to those who would prefer to see a little of how it is done. As we move through the making of a Harrison blank we will learn a little more about test-curve and how it is measured; we'll know a little more of what the spine is and how to find it. And we will see how important the action of a Barbel rod becomes when put into fish-playing practice. The segment will then conclude with some useful tips on how to custom-build our very own rod, for this is one of the most personally rewarding (and surprisingly easy) things that we could do.

RAW MATERIALS

Harrison's buy in carbon fibre in a form known as prepreg. This is short for pre-impregnated. Simply, the carbon fibre arrives as a wide tape on a roll with fibres and resin mixed in metered quantities. Carbon fibre alone is a black floss-like material, very vulnerable to abrasion and damage in its raw state. It's only the combination with a resin system into a composite that makes it a useful engineering material. It's expensive stuff. A 50.m roll can cost thousands of pounds, and Harrison's consume kilometres of it each month. The resin, a modified epoxy system, doesn't cure at room temperature, but needs heat to solidify.

Currently one of the bigger non-aerospace users of prepreg in the UK, Harrisons believe that the material they buy is the best available. It is not the cheapest, but it is the flattest, most consistent, gap free prepreg available, and for that they pay a slight price premium. Their current number one supplier is Cytec Aerospace with whom they work closely on product development. Cytec also supplies into Ferrari, Boeing, McClaren, BMW and many more.

Carbon fibres come in a variety of types, the most commonly used being, M55, M40, M40J, M46J, T300, HR40, a long list. The different types have varying properties when used in a composite. They vary in their modulus and strength. Modulus is, in effect, 'stretchiness.' It is different to strength but can easily be confused. When you make a composite using high modulus fibres, you make a stiff tube or rod. Once you make a high strength tube it may bend more, but it will bend further before failing.

Fishing rods across a wide range of applications need high strength, high modulus and intermediate fibres to perform well. No one fibre is superior. High modulus, though often more expensive, is less preferable than cheaper fibre in some applications. Dr Harrison tends to be somewhat vague on exactly where his company uses different fibres for two reasons. Firstly, he believes they are ahead of the game and does not want to assist his competitors. Secondly, it is almost meaningless to many anglers, as what counts most to us is the rod's performance.

BLANK MANUFACTURE AND DESIGN

As I felt that he would best convey a much fuller understanding of the complexity within this whole operation; I turned to the rod building ingenuity of the man him self, Dr Steve Harrison. Here's what he had to say.

"Design is the first step. That is the most secret bit here, but one important ingredient is experience. There are a small handful of really knowledgeable quality blank makers in the world. We are one of them, and it was hard work getting there! I'm sorry, not too much information is public domain here. I can tell you that we sometimes start with a blank sheet of paper, but more often we take an existing blank and play around with it. Unlike those companies sourcing their rods in the Far East, we have total control. We can go through a cycle of design to prototype in two hours. The importers tell you it took two years to develop a new rod, when most of that time was probably spent waiting for samples. We can develop a rod here in two hours. But then we test it for months.

A design has to be translated into a pattern. Like a dress design, three-dimensional tube starts out as two-dimensional pattern. The patterns are cut by hand from the prepreg. A rod section may be made from one simple wedge shaped pattern, or more often a complex lay up of irregular shapes and different materials. The subtleties of design make the difference. The little changes in taper, stiffening the balance of materials.

An analogy for this can be found in hi-fi. You can take a budget priced system, and with well matched components, good quality cable, interconnects, vibration isolation and electrical supply, make it sound better than a thoughtlessly installed system costing twice the price.

The other variable besides materials is the mandrel, the tapered rod around which the tube is formed. We have a large stock of mandrels of various tapers and size. These are made to our specification in America. We have a large number of each type, as it is uneconomic to make rods one at a time, we have to work in batches.

The mandrels are cleaned and prepared with a releasing agent, then the carbon prepreg pattern is rolled around it using a pneumatic rolling table. It's like rolling a giant tapered cigarette. After rolling, the prepreg is wound under controlled tension with a high performance heat shrinkable tape. This binds the prepreg tight to the mandrel and controls the pressure during cure. The pressure is required to control resin flow, exclude air and make a high performance composite.

The wrapped part is then placed in a curing oven for a period during which the resin is activated, gels, and cures. Cure time is dependent on pattern size, temperature and resin system. A control cycle is measured in hours rather than minutes. On finishing the cure cycle the mandrel is then extracted pneumatically then unwrapped and forwarded to the finishing department. Blanks may be linished using our taper sensing centreless machine, or they may go straight to trimming and jointing.

The linishing is a process used to give a smooth finish and key for painting. About half our blanks are coated with colour finishes, and about half go out with a natural unground finish. Linishing is a simple but critical process. We have the best machinery and graduate level staff on this job. Our technician weighs blanks to check that the minimum of material is removed and no significant alteration to action is made.

Rod sections are fitted together after precision centreless grinding of the male end of one section to fit the female of the section above. Blanks are then ready for building.
This is a very simple account of what we do. The excellence is in the raw materials, the design and finally the subtleties within production. Our staff turnover is nil, our team ambitious and dedicated. It all adds up to a better fishing rod." **Dr Steve Harrison**

My thanks go to Dr Harrison for explaining the blank making process so clearly.

TEST CURVE MEASUREMENT

One of the first questions we ask about a prospective new rod will often relate to its test curve. Many of us do this automatically without really understanding how it is measured or what it really means. We merely assume that because a rod is labelled with our idea of what is correct, it has to be exactly what we are looking for.

Test curve is a measurement that has been used as an indicative guide to a rod's power and action since probably as long ago as the 1950s. Richard Walker is believed to have made one of the first references to it in his book, Stillwater Angling. Test curve is understood to be the weight, in pounds and ounces, that is needed to pull the rod tip round to form a 90-degree angle to the butt. Just like the length of the rod, it is handy to have a measurement that tells us something about its power, even if only limited.

The easiest way to measure test curve is to clamp the rod by its handle in a horizontal position, a few feet from the ground. With line threaded through the rings, a weight is attached close to the tip ring. Starting off with 1.Lb on a rod assumed to be 1.5.Lb TC. The rod will now bend under the weight with a curve developing throughout its length. The test curve is then reached by adding smaller increments of weight until the tip is at right angles to the butt.

The problem with measuring test curve is that the whole process is flawed. As there is no standard way of clamping the handle during measurement, even the slightest change of position here can make vast differences at the tip. This can be felt merely by holding the rod in our hands, as the further back we grip the handle the faster the rod will meet 90-degrees. The outcome of this experiment can be seen far more easily on a rod that has sliding reel fits. By altering the reel's position we can actually increase or decrease the test curve.

ACTIONS SPEAK LOUDER THAN TEST CURVES

Much more important than test curve is the rod's performance and the point at which it assumes the roll of playing the fish. In the event that the rod has an over forgiving action, the weight applied to it by a hooked fish is transferred much too quickly to the butt section, therefore tiring the angler's arm far more quickly than the Barbel. During the realities of fish playing practice, rods of this nature appear almost as though they have no tip section, as most of their test curve is met with the often-savage bite.

What we are ideally looking for is a far steadier, more evenly distributed and progressive build up of the rod's power after the bite occurs. For total efficiency, we need the rod to begin playing the fish as quickly as possible, ideally, after the first 20 inches or so. We want the weight transference to be more balanced throughout the whole length of the blank. That way, we take the fight to the Barbel, not the other way around. These important differences in action can be seen in the diagram below. Top = too forgiving. Bottom action is ideal.

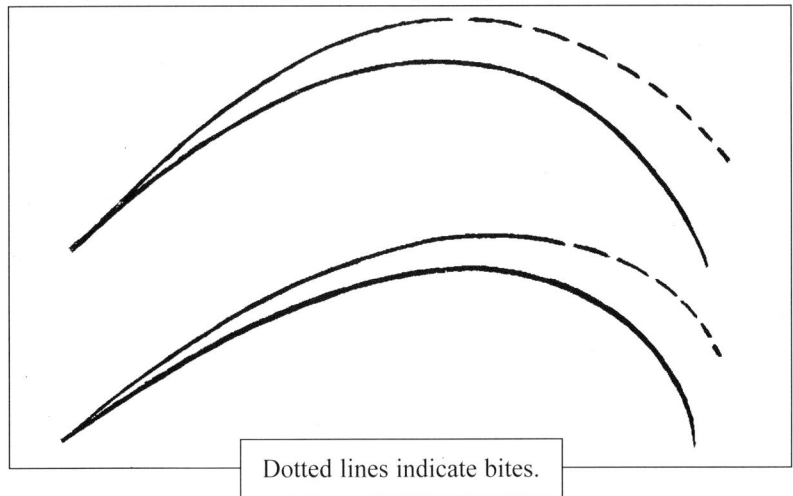

Dotted lines indicate bites.

SPINES

As we have seen, blanks are made by rolling a pattern around a mandrel. As there is a beginning and an end to this process, they can produce both a hard and a soft side to the blank. If we roll a blank while slightly bent, there can be a feeling of a change in stiffness in one part of it. This is what rod manufacturers often refer to as the spine.

If we hold the tip in one hand and twist with the other whilst keeping the rod bent, we are most likely to feel this. Often the spine tends to coincide with a slight bend in the blank, as it tends to pull a slight curve during cure. One of the clearest ways to see this is to rotate the blank section over a large flat surface, such as a kitchen worktop.

Many rod builders will find the stiffest side of the blank, mark it and put the rings 180-degrees in relation to it.

It is very easy for the would-be rod builder to develop hang-ups about the spine, but I would urge you not to worry about it. Ignorance of the spine is something that goes on in lots of rod building factories on a daily basis. By far the easiest thing for the do-it-yourself builder to do is to first put the blank together, then rotate and adjust the sections until the rod is as straight as possible, with any natural curvature in the blank bending upwards, then fit the rings to the underside.

CUSTOM BUILDING

Well, now that we understand a little more about test curves and actions, rod-blank building and the spine that this process often creates, perhaps it's now time to consider finishing a rod all by ourselves. While we cannot improve the Barbel taming qualities contained within the Harrison blank, we can at least make our own personal adjustments to the factory build specification, while at the same time gaining a great deal of satisfaction by doing so.

I think it right to say that we all take a fair amount of pleasure from the first Big Barbel we land on any new rod, but believe me, this pleasure is increased many times when it's a rod you have built yourself. It's unlikely to save you much money, but you will enjoy owning a unique rod that is built to your very own requirements. Anyone can make a decent job of building a rod; it will just take a bit more care and a lot more time for the beginner.

There are a few things that will help. You need a sharp blade, such as a Stanley-knife or scalpel. A cigarette lighter or matches, a roll of good quality 1 inch wide masking tape, a sheet of coarse, medium and smooth emery cloth or sandpaper, good quality whipping thread in a colour of your choice. A pack of Araldite original glue, (not rapid set) clear nail-varnish, (optional) Seymo quick-pro epoxy finish or Yacht-varnish, handle material, (cork or duplon, fixed seat or sliding reel fits) a hook-keeper ring, beta-light attachment and, of course, your rod rings. An empty 'shoe-size' cardboard box with 'V' shaped notches cut into it, a bottle of Tipex correction fluid and permanent black marker pen will also come in handy.

BUILDING THE HANDLE

Assuming that you have decided on which side of the blank the rings are going (see spine) and marked all of the sections, (using tipex) it is now time to build the handle. A length of 21 to 23 inches on 11.ft or 23 to 25 inches on a 12.ft rod is about right.

This example refers to full cork with sliding reel-fits on a blank that is unground.

Take the butt-section and mark the length at which you want the handle to finish. (Using white correction fluid makes the marks easier to remove once the rod is complete). Now take a piece from the sheet of sandpaper and roughen up the unground finish that will be hidden by the cork. This will assist a good bondage of the adhesive. Take care not to scratch the blank above the point where the handle will finish.

Now wipe the excess dust away with a damp cloth and then dry. The inner diameter of the length of cork will be greater than the outer diameter of the handle end of the blank. The difference is made up by tightly winding the correct amount of masking tape around the blank until a tight fit is achieved. A one eighth of an inch gap should be left between each coil of masking tape. This will ensure any excess adhesive has somewhere to go once the handle is glued into position. Choosing a high quality cork will reduce any of the problems associated with this process. Whole handle sections can be purchased, but will need to be cut and trimmed to fit by using your Stanley knife.

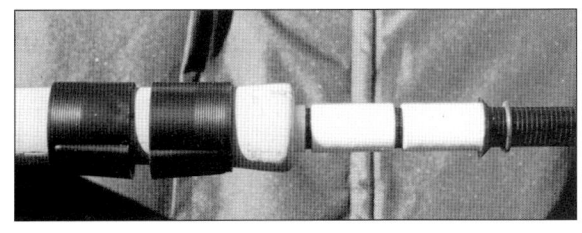

Once a snug fit is achieved down the whole length of the handle, (this may take some time) it is now time to mix the Araldite as instructed on the pack. About one quarter of each tube should be sufficient. Spread the adhesive as evenly as possible along each individual section of masking tape and slide the cork (with reel fits attached) into place, rotating it slightly as you go along. Remove any excess glue and use this to re-attach the trimmed down cork section that you removed earlier. Attaching a handle collar, or even a rubber o-ring to seal the gap at the front will then complete the job. Leave the section to dry over night and then smooth over any joints in the cork with medium and then fine sandpaper. To ensure that the reel fits slide freely, you may also need to sand the handle in this area.

RING POSITIONING

Ask the manufacture for ring spacing. If you want to make adjustments to this, then try any new positions by first taping the rings in place with insulation tape. Try to avoid adding to the number of rings specified by the manufacturer, as this will add more weight to the blank and may even soften it. Be aware that the rod is designed to perform in a specific fashion and that during development ring spacing is likely to have been adjusted a number of times already.

RING PREPARATION

Having already marked the position of the rings onto the blank, it is now time to prepare the ring feet for whipping. This ring preparation is important as it can make the difference between a neat and a messy job.

Rings leave the factory ready to use, but a little grinding and filing will make the job of whipping them on far easier. Make sure that every foot tapers down finely to the blank, that there is no step and no burs. Once this is done, blacken the shiny finish with the permanent marker to hide any gaps that may appear in the whipping.

TYING ON A RING

1. Place your first ring in its position on and tape on one leg to hold it in place. Use masking tape for this.

2. Trap the end of the thread in place by rotating the rod a few times and whipping over the loose end.

3. Cut off any excess of loosely hanging thread.

4. Rotate the rod with one hand and guide the thread with the other.

5. When the thread has almost covered the ring foot, take a loop of spare thread and whip over it. The final 8 turns is about right.

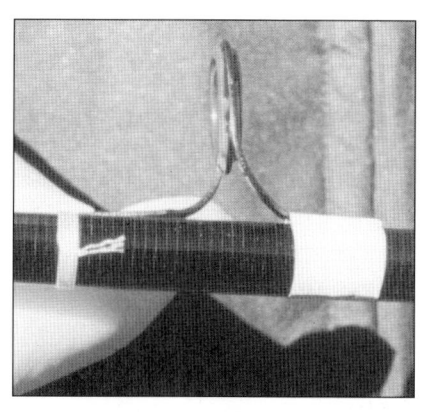

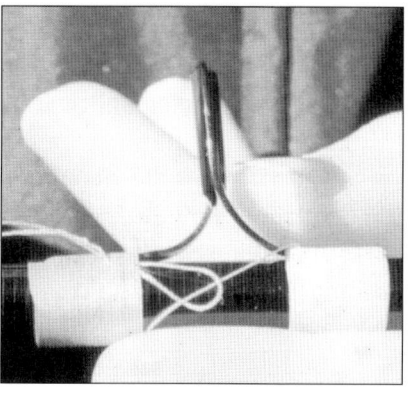

6. Cut the thread going to the spool and pass it through the loop you have just whipped over.

7. Using the loop, pull the cut end of the thread back through the whippings.

8. Trim with a sharp blade.

9. Remove the tape from the other foot, and now repeat.

Points to watch.

Try and keep the tension constant whilst tying the thread.

Avoid gaps as you go, but small gaps can be closed up later using something smooth and cylindrical.

After trimming you can get rid of 'stick-ups' by passing a naked flame quickly over the whipping to singe them off.

FITTING TIP RINGS

These are glued in place and then a whipping for decoration is usually applied. Try always to use two-pack epoxy. (Araldite) Do not use superglue, as it does not like water! Also, tube sizes are rarely exactly right for the tip. If the gap is too big to be filled with glue, use a layer of whipping thread to build the tip up.

WHIPPING JOINTS

It as always been common practice to whip over the female end of joints and over areas where spigots are glued. These days, most rod joints have sufficient reinforcement within the blank, but a whipping always puts a finishing touch to any such area.

VARNISHING

Once all the rings and other whippings are in place, the next step is varnishing. Seymo quick-pro epoxy is ideal for this, as it offers the amateur a professional type finish. Prior to epoxy arriving on the scene, all rods were built using traditional yacht type varnish. This air dries slowly and will need several more coats than epoxy to give a decent finish, but it still remains a good option for the amateur. It is at this point that the cardboard box is used to both assist application and support the sections whilst drying.

This is the trickiest part of the whole operation, therefore I would urge you to practice on an old rod or garden cane with a ring tied on.

TIP. Whippings can first be sealed with a thin coat of clear nail-varnish, in preference to the Seymo PVA sealer contained within the pack.

Follow the manufacturer's instructions for mixing the epoxy and apply with a brush that does not lose hairs. Paint the resin on taking care only to put it on the whippings, as it will be difficult to remove any unwanted excess from the blank. A blast of warm air from a hair-drier will make the resin less viscous and easier to apply. But be careful about excess heat, as it will reduce the pot life of the epoxy.

TIP. A rough guide is that for every increase in temperature of 10 C, the curing time will be halved.

Whilst you are coating the whippings, keep the rod section turning in your hand, as this will prevent runs from developing. Finish each whipping with a small spot of resin applied to the angle between the ring leg and the blank. A quick blast from the hair-drier whilst rotating the rod will make the resin flow into one clear smooth coating. You must ensure that you keep the blank turning all the time you are working.

CURING

Finished sections should be cured in a warm and dust free room. As each section is finished, place into the slots within the cardboard box and rotate it at intervals. As the section is rotated, sags or runs that are developing will run back. Regular rotation will result in a run free professional job. Initially, you need to rotate the section every few minutes. Room temperatures effect this greatly, so you will have to check your work regularly. In a warm room, you will soon be able to extend the intervals between rotations.

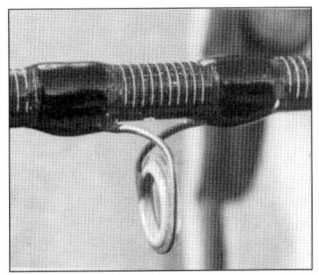

Under warm conditions, one thick coat of epoxy varnish should be alright to be left alone after about two hours. However, you may choose to build the Seymo finish in stages by applying thinner coats, in which case a one-hour checking time will be fine. When building up the finish in this way, leave a minimum of 12 hours between coats. (Yacht varnish can also be used in this way). Full cure of epoxy can take between a day and a week. Do not let the job go suddenly cold or expose it to high humidity before full cure, as this will cause a bloom. The result should resemble that in the above photo!

TIP. If the finished job is slightly soft or sticky, an extra coat will help to activate the cure in the layer below.

Excess resin can be removed with cellulose thinners or nail-varnish remover, but these can damage the gloss finish on painted blanks. Test any thinner on a small area of the blank first. For your very first build job, an unground natural finished blank is the number one choice.

Note! Although Harrison's do not deal directly with the angling public, anyone wishing to purchase their blanks and many of the accessories needed for DIY rod building can do so by ordering from their nearest Harrison stockist.

CHAPTER 3 BAITS

INTRODUCTION
MAGGOTS AND CASTERS
CORN
MEAT
HEMP
CHEESE
WORMS
MINNOWS
MEALWORMS
DESIGNER BASE MIXES
FLAVOURINGS AND ADDITIVES
THE ULTIMATE DESIGNER

INTRODUTION TO BAITS AND TACTICS

The rules of Barbel angling are set in stone, Right? – Wrong! It doesn't seem so long ago that the only way to capture these amazing creatures was to adhere to the guidelines set down in some 'how-to where-to' rule book. How things have changed!

By now we should all be aware of the tactical changes and the so-called bait revolution that seem destined to alter our particular branch of the sport. And whether we like it or not, sooner or later the traditionalists split cane rod and centre-pin approach will become even more pre-historic than it already is.

To a certain extent I can understand the horror that the ardent traditionalist sees whilst witnessing these changes. But the fact remains that split cane rods, two rods per swim, boilies, hair-rigs, popcorn, flavoured baits, designer pastes, high-pitched optonics and noisy centre-pin ratchets, all come under the umbrella of present day Barbel angling. Whether one chooses to move with these changes is entirely down to individual choice. From a purely personal point of view, I feel that if we ignore them completely our fishing will undoubtedly be suffering whilst we remain unaware of it. Equally, to adopt any one single-minded approach, such as using what could only be described as carp tactics for Barbel, will inevitably result in the same outcome.

The wiser choice must surely be for us to move with the changes, and decide which of the older and more modern tactics we could combine and adapt to our own personal approach. Only then can we be certain that we are fishing the water of our choice in the most proficient way that we can.

At this particular moment in time, I suppose I would label myself a modern traditionalist, who has found the right personal balance of baits and tactics, both old and new, and applied them directly to the capture of the bigger specimens. If there is one thing that I have learned above all else over the last few years, it is that meticulous attention to detail is absolutely vital to achieving consistent big fish results.

The next two chapters of the book are entirely devoted to showing you exactly what these baits and tactics are, and this will serve as an introduction to both.

MAGGOTS AND CASTERS

While maggots and casters are both superb Barbel baits in their own right; their one major drawback is that they are too attractive to many other species, especially in summer. During these warmer months of the season, using either of these baits in a selective fashion can prove a very expensive task, as it is not unusual to have to use a gallon or more per session. Not very cost effective when at least half of that quantity is wasted on nuisance fish. Still, if money is no object, then the use of either bait can offer us one of the most devastatingly effective ways of catching Big Barbel in warm, gin-clear water.

During the winter months, while casters often become a less effective option, the maggot comes into its own. By far the best way of using maggots in cold water is to use them dead – either gassed, or heavily flavoured and frozen preferably – but most definitely, Dead! If you are in no position to kill them in this manner, then pouring boiling water on to them just before you go fishing will do the trick.

You can always dunk them in a flavour on the bank. (See tactics for freezing and gassing) It has always remained one of Barbel fishing's great mysteries why dead maggots are so effective in winter. I suspect it is because the fish prefer softer baits at this time of year, but whatever the reason, dead maggots in winter are often selective of the bigger fish when used as described in the tactical section.

CORN

Tinned sweetcorn kernels have been successful as Barbel bait for years. In clear water conditions their natural bright yellow colour makes them easily visible whilst lying on the riverbed. This is a huge advantage to the specimen Barbel hunter, as it allows us to observe the rate at which the food is being consumed. In exceptionally clear water, 'corn watching' allows us the added luxury of being able to move the bait from the path of an unwanted fish, such as a smaller Barbel or much worse, a chub! Corn is now available in a variety of different colours and by far the best when fishing blindly is black. When used in conjunction with large quantities of hemp, black corn can be a superbly selective bait. Adding salt and sugar to any colour corn will often make it even more effective.

MEATS

Although a great deal of experimentation is possible with the many different varieties of meats available at the supermarket delicatessen, it is tinned meats that remain the first choice of many anglers, luncheon meat being the most popular. This is arguably the number one most successful Big Barbel bait in history and, along with chopped ham and pork, and bacon grill, still offers the angler one of the most selective ways in which we can fish – The Big Bait Method. (See tactics)

Even when not fished in such large pieces, on their day, all of these meats can still be deadly effective. And once flavouring and colouring are considered the most devastating options for these baits become fully unleashed. Whilst colouring these most popular of meat-baits should become almost standard practice in those areas where the Barbel become instantly spooked at the sight of them in their normal state, also adding flavour gives them extra pulling power both at night and in coloured water.

HEMPSEED

The Barbel attractive qualities of the cooked hemp-seeds' aroma are such that it can draw fish upstream by a distance of 50 yards or more. Therefore it must remain part of our optional fishing bait armoury if we are to enjoy continued success, especially whilst tackling a number of different venues throughout the course of a season. Hemp has a habit of being more effective in some areas than others, even on the same river, and so if possible it often pays dividends to check with anglers who are already fishing the stretch whether it is worth our while carrying it with us.

We should also consider that in some instances, certain individual specimens may refuse to feed over large quantities of hemp that suddenly crash onto the riverbed. In this situation, it's more likely the sight of the seed mass rather than their aroma that the fish feel wary of. Should we experience this, or suspect that it could be happening, we could always explore the options outlined in the tactical section. We could also try the excellent parti-blend from Hinders of Swindon. This is a mixture of hemp and other seed particles and makes a very attractive alternative.

CHEESE

Cheese is undoubtedly one of the most productive Barbel baits that we could choose to use. However, as many of us are also aware of the chubs' liking for it, this is undoubtedly a reason why we so rarely attempt to use it. If the Barbel population is the more dominant within our stretch, then we are far better to make cheese one of our primary bait options.

As is often the case with any non-natural bait that is made in a variety of different ways, and with different ingredients, certain particular cheeses are more effective than others. Usually it is those smellier cheeses with higher fat content that the Barbel find the most attractive, with Danish blue being among the best. Although exceptionally good as a night-time summer bait, cheese becomes more effective during the colder months.

A problem normally associated with certain cheeses at this time of year is that they often become too hard. This can be overcome in the case of blue cheese by mixing it with ready-made shortcrust pastry mix, thawed straight from the freezer. Use this at one part pastry mix to three parts cheese. Strong mature cheddar can also be added to blue cheese, mixed at 50/50 before adding the pastry. A heaped teaspoon of hot chilli powder and some red or black colouring also make good additions to the paste.

SCENTS AND 'SCENTSABILITY'

Evolution has equipped the Barbel with a sense of smell many thousands of times more acute than that of our own. Many of us suspect that by using this highly developed sense that not only can the Barbel home in on a particular scent, but that it can also seek out life-supporting nutrients such as amino and organic acids, sodium and fats, etc. If the fish really are capable of searching for food in such an analytical way, then this may explain why certain cheeses are instantly attractive to them. Could it really be nothing more than sheer coincidence that those cheeses which are usually the most productive are not only the smelliest, but are often also the ones with high fat and sodium content?

As the Barbel prepare for their colder water, slower metabolic rate, they seek to pack on weight during the months of the autumn. When readying themselves for this form of semi-hibernation, it is almost as though they instantly foresee the potential food value within the cheese. This is only theory of course, as the Barbel themselves are the only ones with all the answers. But, it would certainly seem that providing our cheese has the correct balance of nutrients, animal fat and a sense appealing aroma, there is no logical reason why the Barbel shouldn't eat it. For whatever the reason that cheese is so effective, it still remains the only non-natural bait that I would expect to be truly instantly effective without prior introduction.

WORMS

During the first major flood of the season, Barbel can often be found extremely close to the bank. This was readily thought to be as a means for them to escape the vast amounts of summer debris that often renders the river un-fishable until it subsides. Nowadays, it is more commonly understood that the Barbel are simply gorging themselves on the feast of lobworms that nature provides for them, not only at this time, but also during the majority of other occasions the river is in flood. It is also worth our while to bear in mind that a well presented lobworm in the clearest of conditions often works where everything non-natural has failed. It therefore makes sense for us to keep the lobworm as a season long bait option, and to perhaps carry at least a few of them with us at all times, especially if we intend to fish during the day.

While the flat-tailed lobworm is always our first choice, in the event that we have problems acquiring them, the more commonly found garden dendrobaena makes an acceptable alternative.

Lobworm collecting is best done on the grassy surface of our local public sports field during the hours of darkness, just after a prolonged spell of rain. It is then that they are more likely to be away from their holes and, in all probability, lying in wait for us to collect them from the wet surface of the grass. To a smaller extent, this method of collection can be artificially re-created on our very own – or friendly neighbours – garden lawn by using a garden hose and/or sprinkler system.

All we need to collect the worms is a good wide-beamed torch, a bucket to put them in, and a stealthy light-footed approach. That way we get the chance to gather them before they disappear back inside their holes, as is sure to happen if we attempt to collect them haphazardly. Failing this, we can always purchase them through mail order, or of course, the tackle shops.

MINNOWS

Throughout the whole summer and well into the autumn, there are periods when Barbel will feed avidly on small fish of many species, but none more so than the minnow. Whether this is because of the minnows' size, texture, or even a combination of both, remains unclear. But, whatever the reason, Barbel quite simply adore them.

The best way to make use of minnows is to use them freshly killed and present them statically on the bottom. In gin-clear water conditions, a dead minnow can also be tantalisingly twitched and manoeuvred to within inches of a target fish that we have spotted from the bank. Used in this way, the Barbel will often respond instantly and savagely, and this can take the unprepared angler by total surprise.

Although some anglers recommend hooking minnows once through the lip, bites are often missed through the sheer speed at which they occur, often resulting in the angler striking before the hook is taken fully into the Barbel's mouth. As they are usually taken tail first, a better option is to hook them once through the back, just above the dorsal fin. Once we become familiar with the Barbels' response to these baits, we will soon realise a little line is best given to allow the fish to take in the hook. Therefore, the strike is best delayed for a couple of seconds longer than usual. In these circumstances, touch legering is also advised.

CADDIS GRUB AND MEALWORMS

Once a shoal of Barbel become pre-occupied with any natural water-born food source, the only way we are allowed to muscle in on their frenzy, is to either use that same food as our hook-bait, or find an acceptable imitation. Caddis grubs are high on the Barbels' favourite food menu, and large numbers of them can be found hiding under the flat edged stones and rocks in the warm clear waters of the shallows during high summer.

However, should we have difficulty collecting the larvae of the sedge fly, a very good imitation is the mealworm as these are often accepted during a caddis grub feast. Mealworms are more conveniently collected, as they can be purchased from the larger pet shops that sell animals of a more exotic nature. While the mealworm makes a Barbel acceptable imitation, its average length of three-quarters of an inch makes it a little larger than the caddis.

DESIGNER BASE MIXES

Although a few of the older 'high nutritional value' carp-bait mixes where used under a blanket of secrecy to catch Barbel for many years, the increasing popularity of the species has led a few commercial bait manufacturers to design these types of base-mixes specifically with Barbel in mind. More commonly referred to as 'designers,' the theory behind these baits is that their ingredients are said to supply all of the nutritional value that the Barbel could require from their diet.

One of the grey areas surrounding the use of these baits is whether they require pre-introduction (pre-baiting). Although the commercial profiteers of designers would prefer us to believe they are instantly attractive to Barbel that have neither seen or eaten them before, many anglers who try them in this way could well be disappointed with the results. Designers undoubtedly work far more effectively once the fish have become accustomed to them; therefore, it is more economical for us to use them in areas where they are already well established.

Unless we need to begin a baiting campaign within an isolated area (see, Into the Wilderness), it is likely that only very little, if indeed any pre-introduction will need to be done. As designers are often heavily used in the more popular venues, Barbel just about everywhere are likely to be already familiar with them. In these instances much of our pre-baiting has been done for us, simply because once the Barbel have become familiar with any one specific designer, they will readily inspect any other which appears similar.

Of the mixes concocted specifically for the species, there are two brands in particular that I would recommend. Although they are not in order of preference, these are

1. John Baker's Search 4 and standard base-mix. Frost and Flood mix for cooler temperatures and/or high water conditions. Full instructions come supplied.

2. Action Baits. Marine Harvest. Oriental Dream. Full instructions come supplied.

Of the mixes originally designed for carp, I have tried only one manufacturer's products – **Rod Hutchinson. 1. Seafood Blend. 2. Super fish and liver. 3. MC mix.** Number four **Addicted**, I believe will go on to become as classic a mix for Barbel as it is proving to be for carp. This is Rod's latest concoction, and I was fortunate to be involved with a little field testing prior to its release. To make a paste with any of Rod's mixes, simply follow the instructions up to the point of boiling.

FLAVOURS AND ADDITIVES

Mr Sceptic: "How do we know whether a Barbel would still have picked up, say, a plain chunk of meat or bunch of maggots, had we not gone to the trouble of flavouring them?"

Even though I have no doubt whatsoever that certain flavours and additives do enhance the appeal of many baits, please allow me to engage you in a story that may well, if you will excuse the pun, offer even the most sceptical amongst us some serious food for thought.

Throughout the early 1990s, I would regularly make the 130 mile round trip from my home to fish either one of two venues located on the middle Severn, around Bridgnorth. At that particular time, dare I say it, I regularly used two rods: one for maggot feeder, the second one for meat. From June 16th until the end of September, for five consecutive seasons, I alternated between the two venues at least three times per week. (I was totally obsessed with banking my first ever double from here and eventually managed to do it with a fish of 10.Lb 1.oz) Although at that time I was using flavours occasionally, I must admit that I was still a little sceptical. Or was it naive?

On this particular day in late August 91, I had made the way to my favourite peg only to find it occupied. Through sheer and hurried excitement, I had left all of my flavoured baits in the freezer, and at that particular time didn't carry any additives with me. As it was such a long walk from the car, I decided to rest for a short while at the top of the high bank behind the angler who was in 'my' swim. Just as I had sat down to regain my breath, I caught the sight of a flashing Barbel: then another and another, and another. For at least a 75-yard stretch immediately downstream of the angler, there were Barbel flashing everywhere. Quite probably, I had underestimated the shoal to contain in excess of 200 fish. I have never - even to this day - seen so many Barbel spread over such a short distance of three tightly packed swims. Even more amazing was the fact that they were all feeding. Head up, belly up, arse up, tail walking, jumping clear of the water like only Barbel and Dolphins do, they were in complete and utter frenzy.

It took me a maximum of three minutes to figure out exactly what was happening and so I turned to the angler and asked if he had caught anything, whilst vainly hoping that he hadn't and that he was going to pack up and leave them all to me. His response soon brought me back down to Earth as he replied, *" I've had my best day ever! Nineteen fish up to now, biggest nine and a half. I wish I could stay a lot longer, but I've got to leave in an hour or so."* I hate to admit it, but I immediately thought - just as most of you lot would - Great! I'll hang on a bit then. No sooner had that thought passed through my mind than he kindly said he didn't mind if I fished the next peg down. *"I hope you've got plenty of white maggots!"* He yelled.

Lucky for me, or so I thought, was that I always took a minimum of three pints of whites for a late afternoon/evening session. Instead of travelling with the maggots cooped up in the boot for an hour and a half, I always purchased them fresh from a tackle-shop in Bridgnorth, just as I had done on this occasion. Six pound Bs mainline tied to a 16 inch 6.Lb low diameter hook-link; double white maggot on a size 16 hook below a 2 oz Drennan feeder was my standard rig in those days. And rather coincidentally, it was an identical set-up to the chap who was bagging the Barbel. Ten minutes later my first cast went in and I anticipated that a bite would soon be forthcoming. Fifteen uneventful minutes later and in went cast number two. In the mean time, the chap in the swim above had taken another two fish and was now on 21.

Another ten minutes passed and I'd not had a knock or a twitch, not even a line bite, and yet our feeders went into the water at no more than six feet apart. I couldn't understand it. Identical set-up, fishing virtually the same swim with the same coloured maggots, no activity on my rod and yet his was jumping about all over the place as the fish attacked his feeder. It just wasn't logical, so I went over to investigate and asked, "You did say *white* maggots, didn't you?"

"I feel a bit guilty now," he said with a grin on his face *"I just had to see it for myself, just to back up what I suspected!"*

"What's that?" I said.

"Well, to tell you the truth, I'd fished the whole morning on plain white maggots and never had a touch," he said, whilst reaching under his tackle-box and producing an almost empty 1 inch high container with a flip-up lid. *"I then dropped this flavour into the maggots and fifteen minutes later began to catch, and I haven't stopped since. The only time I can't get a bite now is if I use plain maggots. Just watch this!"*

He then proceeded to fill his feeder and bait his hook with unflavoured maggots, and then cast in. Nothing happened. Not a twitch for five minutes, so he reeled in and changed to flavoured maggots, then re-cast to the same spot. No more than twenty seconds passed before his quiver tip was again bouncing all over the place. Two minutes later all the activity stopped, as there was nothing left in the feeder. Half a minute on, the tip heaved round and he was into Barbel number 22, which I gladly netted for him.

"Is that the only place in the swim you can get a bite?" I asked.

"NO!" he responded, *"I get bites much quicker there, but I can get them anywhere I cast; watch!"*

He then re-filled with flavoured maggots and cast 25 yards upstream, a total of around 40 yards from the most productive spot. It took about two or three minutes for the fish to respond as the rod tip changed from completely still to the usual twitching and dancing quiver that I had witnessed from every cast he'd made since my arrival – with the only exception being plain white maggots. The sudden appearance of slack line and a straight quiver indicated a drop-back bite and he was again attached to a fish.

By this time I was so intrigued by it all that I stayed with him until he packed in. He finished with 27 Barbel - with at least 10 losses, but not before another couple of demonstrations that the fish would not accept the bait without flavour. He even tried my freshly bought maggots that carried not a hint of sweat-induced ammonia. He had begun fishing at 10.30am and fished until about 3.00pm without so much as a knock. He then added the flavour to his maggots and, around 3.15pm, cast back in.

From 3.30ish until 6.30pm – when he left me with enough bait for 2 or 3 casts and a virtually empty bottle with only a couple of drops of flavour in the bottom – he had hooked no fewer than 37 Barbel. All of them on flavoured white maggots. None whatsoever took plain ones. As for myself, I managed to catch five fish during the first hour of him leaving, the last bite coming at about 8.00pm and coinciding with my last feeder full of flavoured maggots. I persevered with the plain maggots, and meat, but to absolutely no avail. When I left at around 9.30, the swim was still alive with Barbel!

While I could easily fill the remainder of the contents of this chapter with numerous similar true stories involving other baits – admittedly to a lesser degree – I feel this one in particular best conveys the point I am trying to make. Of course, we must all realise this story does not prove that flavours work. But even the most sceptical amongst us should also take into account that it most certainly gives us no indication that they do not.

The author with a middle-Severn 'scraper' double of 10lb 1oz.

SNIFFING OUT THE ANNUALS

I dare say that once any Barbel angler becomes accustomed to the benefits of using bait additives he will always have his particular favourites. Once he has gained that all-important confidence that they can undoubtedly promote, he may be tempted to stay with one particular brand name or manufacturer's products. Over the course of a few seasons, he may well have extended the number of his 'old favourites' to say, half a dozen or so. He should also have gained both the knowledge and experience of when and where to use any one in particular.

Some additive manufacturers claim that a particular flavour that is good in warm water is not so good in winter and vice-versa. While this may well be true of some, (and could be substantiated by the findings of many anglers – including my own) it is my belief that there are, and always have been, more singular additives than we may imagine that are highly capable of producing fish the whole season through.

Usually, the very best additives around actually possess this capability and the only difference between their individual effectiveness in either summer or winter is dependent only upon the dosage used. Providing that we are tuned into the appropriate levels of water temperature at which to make the necessary adjustments all should be fine. As a rule of thumb, although this may vary slightly depending on the product, my own recommendation is that for every 1.ml of flavour you are successful with in water temperatures above 12 degrees Celsius, try adding half ml extra in temperatures below this – down to 9 degrees; adding a further half ml in even colder water. Therefore effectively doubling the warmer dosage for the winter conditions. These guidelines are certainly a good starting point for the many existing carp-bait flavours that appear only to carry instructions for base-mixes. In the event that you are using additives designed specifically for Barbel, you should find that clearly defined instructions for use are marked somewhere upon the packaging.

My recommendations for flavours/additives are as listed below. (s) Denotes recommended for use in summer only. (sw) for both summer and winter. (w) Winter.

Rod Hutchinson. (s) Scopex. Esterfruit. Strawberry cream. (sw) Hemp. Mega-spice. Spicy liver sausage. Spice sense appeal. Monster crab. The liver. Secret Agent.

Archie Braddock. (s) Floral surprise. Fruit surprise. Barbel Magic summer. (sw) Spice surprise. Mandarin Plus. (w) Hot Magic. Barbel Magic winter.

John Baker. (sw) Search 4. Frost and Flood. Meatball.

Action Baits. (sw) Sausage Sizzle.

Seer Products. (sw) Liquid Frenzy.

THE ULTIMATE DESIGNER

I wonder what the majority of us would do given that they were in my position. For a little over two years now, I have been experimenting with what I now refer to as The Ultimate Designer. Consistent results over this sustained period leave me to assume that I'm currently sitting on what may be a highly significant development in bait design. Only you, the angling public as a whole, can truly decide whether I am right or wrong. If I am wrong then it won't be for the first time and I'll take it like a man. Please bear with me!

Not so long ago, I would have found it extremely difficult to keep my experiments under wraps. But thankfully my brief and now discontinued enterprise in commercial bait flavouring manufacture has taught me a few harsh lessons in the importance of secrecy. Or rather, who to tell and who not to tell, and of course what to tell when I choose to say anything at all. Nevertheless, I am willing to share some of the basic principles of the Ultimate Designer's development and preparation, and I have been asked to make it available for others to explore the many different options for its full potential. Two of those options include making the concept available to the angling public in both kit-form and tinned ready-made baits. As yet I remain undecided which, if any option to take.

This is not the whole story as that could easily take the entire contents of a book to cover; in addition, I am not going to give all my secrets away! However, what I can reveal now is that by making up a binder using three separate ingredients, I can take virtually any non-natural bait, cook, enhance and re-form it. I can also mix a multitude of different types of bait together, re-form, colour and flavour them the whole way through if I wish. The finished texture of the product resembles that of luncheon meat and so can be cut or torn from a block to any size or shape required.

High protein fish pellets, designer base mixes, tinned hot-dog sausages, peperami, meatballs, corned beef; all of these and many more different ingredients I have successfully re-formed; used either combined or singly. Even cooked hempseed can be used and cut to whatever size is chosen.

As you can see, the application of this bait lends itself to a wide range of uses, and although I have revealed only a little about my experiments, it shouldn't be difficult for anyone to imagine the potential involved here. Moreover, not only with Barbel, but the majority of other freshwater species also. Over two year's research and development have left me with a good number of tried and tested recipes. But it becomes abundantly clear through the available exploitation of so many different individual ingredients that the permutations for making unique baits are virtually endless. It certainly adds to the option of wrapping a paste around a boilie!

Designed on fishmeal pellets above. Here, just under actual size!

Traditional flavoured meat baits or conventional designer pastes will always continue to catch some very big fish, particularly when the Barbel have become habituated to living off anglers baits in preference to natural food. But my results over the last few seasons indicate that there may be a better way to make baits that will bank more Big Barbel more often. Perhaps including those big, beautiful, natural specimens that are seldom seen or caught.

These photos, plus the one in the colour section, could be a glimpse of the future. Just remember where you saw it first! See future editions of the weekly Angling press for possible further information.

CHAPTER 4

TACTICS

SUMMER

TWO RODS: ONE HOOK
SIGHT SELECTION
CHOPPED MAGGOTS AND CASTERS
TOUCH LEGERING
FLAVOURING AND FREEZING MAGGOTS
GASSED MAGGOTS
THE BIG-BAIT METHOD
HAIR RIGGING – THE HAIR AND THE NEEDLE
BAITS ON ELASTIC
HEMP BOMBS
INTO THE WILDERNESS
THE THREE-SWIM ROTATION SYSTEM
ROUTINE MAINTENANCE
DEMORALISATION
RETURNING TO BASICS

Although many of us become thoroughly excited at the prospect that yet another magical June 16th is to break our three-month long lay-off, it is not uncommon for the Barbel population within many rivers to appear completely unimpressed with the amount of different baits we begin to throw at them.

Barbel are notoriously one of the season's slowest starters and we can be two or three weeks into any new season before any consistent response is given to our baits. It is widely assumed that this varying response-rate is down to a number of factors such as how, when, and if at all the Barbel have spawned, and of course their three-month lack of familiarity with any non-natural food source.

While the fish themselves are again in possession of all the answers, I cannot help but imagine that a fair amount of the whole picture can be drawn from both theories. Even more so from the theory on baits, as there is very little doubt that naturals such as lobworms and minnows will account for far more fish than non-naturals during this period. This three-month natural diet will also include a vast amount of smaller foods such as caddis-grub and freshwater shrimps, and this is quite possibly a reason why the Barbel do eventually show a more rapid response to the anglers' particle-baits such as maggots, corn, and in particular, casters.

TWO RODS: ONE HOOK

On the majority of Barbel rivers it is casters which become more rapidly accepted. Whether or not this is because so many anglers prefer to use them early season remains unclear, but whatever the reason, more Big Barbel fall to casters than any other particle-bait at the onset of the season – especially when fished in conjunction with a feeder. However, once we pass mid-July, the bigger fish appear to wise up to these tactics and are less likely to be captured using them. Even so, there is a way in which the feeder can remain useful to the specimen hunter until well into the autumn.

   I am a firm believer in the popular theory that, once they have wised up, the bigger fish will often hang back from a feeder and selectively pick off hook-free samples a good way downstream. The two-rod, one hook method is something which has enforced my belief in this theory even further. The idea behind it is to use one rod to cast out the feeder (without a hook-link) at the regular intervals normally associated with the standard method, and to use a second rod with a baited hook on a running-leger rig 15 or 20 yards below it. The bait can be either a bunch of casters, or a large lump of flavoured meat, preferably hair-rigged. I first began using this method on the middle Severn a number of years ago and have also achieved a fair amount of success while using it on both the Dove and the Trent.

SIGHT SELECTION

One of the most exciting ways to catch Big Barbel is to fish for them by sight. Obviously, our initial and often most problematic area of location is more easily solved when our venue is blessed with a high degree of water clarity. This offers us the wonderful opportunity to observe, say, a small group of Barbel and selectively pick out a specific target fish of our choice. By observing the whole group's behaviour and response to the introduction of food, we can then build up a picture of each individual member's habitual pattern of feeding and carefully time the introduction of our hook-bait accordingly.

However, while this is often one of the most devastatingly effective methods that we can choose to adopt, it could also be rather expensive. As the most effective baits are maggots or casters with hemp, it is not uncommon for us to require a gallon or more per session. As it usually takes us a considerable amount of time to build up the swim, we should note that a great deal of patience and self-control are required if we are to be successful. This method often requires that we introduce free samples of food at regular intervals lasting for a period of anything between 3 and 6 hours before introducing a hook-bait. The way in which we prepare the swim is crucial to any success, and just one momentary lapse of concentration on our part can result in spooking the fish.

If we have located a group of Barbel and can keep our waterside presence totally inconspicuous, we should prepare the swim from a position that's preferably no closer than 15 yards upstream of them. A patch of clean gravel that's no more than a few feet square and also close to our own bank is ideal. Providing we have plenty of bank-side cover, we then need to introduce our particle baits via a bait-dropper at between 6 and 10 dropper loads. These should be consecutively lowered (not cast) into the swim as rapidly as possible and the swim topped up every 30 minutes or so.

Because of their instinctive caution, it is common for the Barbel to vacate the area after the initial introduction of any bait, and we need only become concerned should they not return within a few minutes. After about an hour or so we should be able to begin a proper observation of their response. By ensuring that we remain stealthy, we can watch how often the target fish visits the feeding area and take note of how long it stays during each visit. These times will vary from not long initially to a little longer each time. It is the fish's natural caution that we need to overcome, and we must keep the food level topped up according to the groups response. Should the swim become devoid of enough food for too long a period, the Barbel are likely to vacate the area completely and not return.

After a period of around three hours observation, we should then have a clear picture of when the target fish is due to enter the area. This is where our patience begins to pay dividends and we can begin to think about introducing a baited hook at a time that coincides with a visit. To reduce the risk of any unwanted fish picking up the bait, this introduction should be made as close to visitation time as possible – even as close as 60 seconds. If we are both patient and lucky enough, the Barbel will be so frenzied by their problem-free feeding spell that we may even catch the entire group by repeating the process after each individual capture. This method also works with hemp and corn, but often considerably less effectively. (See hook-links and rigs.)

Another way to use the method, while at the same time saving ourselves a little time and money, is to prepare the swim later in the day, with our only intention being to fish during the hours of darkness. Two hours of feeding the swim in exactly the same way before the onset of dusk is ideal. Although we'll be unable to observe the fish once darkness falls, their natural daytime caution should have been completely abandoned by this time, and they are more likely to remain within the swim until every morsel of food has been consumed.

Because of the potential daytime expense involved with this tactic, it is quickly adopting the label as the method that buys you fish. It therefore pays those of us on a tight budget to note that Big Barbel can be captured far more easily and often considerably less expensively, during the hours of darkness – providing the venue's controlling club permits this of course!

CHOPPED MAGGOTS AND CASTERS

During many instances while using maggots and casters, it's possible that at least two or three pints of bait will need to be introduced before the Barbel respond. It is far more likely we will attract the attentions of mass quantities of minnows and other small species initially. Many anglers believe that when maggots/casters are used as bait, it is often the activity of these smaller fish that provokes the Barbels' response. Whilst I go along with this theory in the main, I feel it's more likely the effect the small fish have on the bait rather than the minnows themselves that arouse the Barbels' interests.

As minnows attack each single maggot or caster the baits inner juices begin to enter the water. Not too rapidly initially, as each single maggot can be seen to have up to half a dozen minnows attached to both ends and midriff. However, once this initial famine-like attitude towards the bait subsides a little, many more maggots are passed around individually and so more amino-laden juices escape into the water.

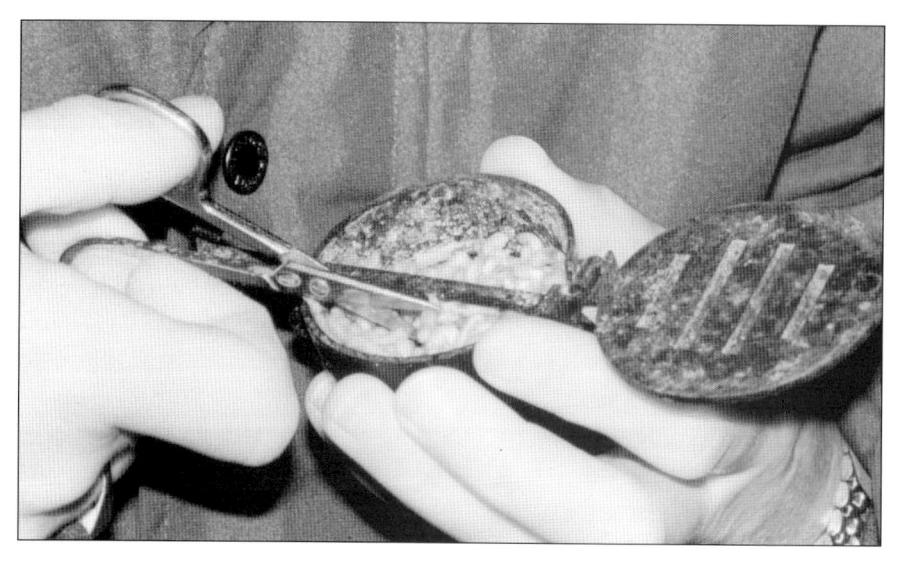

A good way for us to promote this process is to introduce some freshly chopped bait. When fishing the method described in sight selection, the last two dropper loads of each top-up are better chopped. To avoid having to handle the mess, simply chop the maggots or casters with your scissors while they are in the dropper. It's also a good idea to do the same when using a swim-feeder – especially when used in conjunction with flavours.

TOUCH LEGERING

Although I have included this technique within the summer tactical section, I appreciate that there are quite a few anglers who prefer to use this method of bite detection throughout the entire duration of the season. Without entering too deeply into the contentious issue of Barbel bites, it could be strongly argued that the art of touch legering offers a far greater conversion ratio of turning bites into fish than any other form of bite indication. Certainly when this ratio is measured against straightforward rod top legering, I would expect the odds to be as high as 3 to 1 in favour of the touch method.

While touch legering is a great method of detecting Barbel bites in their many forms, I believe its truest value is to be experienced when using big baits. As fishing with such baits commonly results in a bite from a Big Barbel, when touch legering the bait can be given to the fish as opposed to the Barbel taking it and bolting away, as is often the case when the fish hooks itself against the rod top. Either that or the bite doesn't develop at all because the Barbel detects the unnatural movement of the bait and so rejects it.

All forms of touch legering are most efficient when using a free running weight. Big baits are best placed in the desired spot and any slack line retrieved. Once this process is achieved, we must then form a loop of approximately six inches of line and hold it between the thumb and index finger of our free hand. The grip that we apply to the line should be no more than is needed to stop the flow of the river from straightening the loop. The bite from a big fish will often be felt as a couple of tugs initially, followed by a firm and positive drawing of line through the fingers. The rod should be kept as low as possible and pointed in the direction of the bait. Once the loop has been pulled through the fingers and the line tightens, a firm, sure and sweeping strike should result in a hooked and completely unsuspecting Big Barbel.

FLAVOURING AND FREEZING MAGGOTS

As previously mentioned in the chapter on baits, flavoured dead maggots are extremely effective Big Barbel baits. The most efficient way to flavour them is to do so while they are still alive and free from any maize meal or similar substance that may be used to keep them dry. First take a large freezer-bag and drop in approximately one and a half-ml of flavour for each pint of maggots (summer). Now add the maggots and blow up the bag with a little air and tie the top of the bag. Let the maggots crawl freely around for fifteen minutes or so, then untie the bag and expel all the air. Now re-tie the bag and place inside a second bag for safe keeping. The maggots are then best placed straight into the freezer, or alternatively kept in a cool, safe place for 24 to 48 hours before use.

GASSED MAGGOTS

Although gassed maggots can be used in a variety of successful ways, the most effective is to use them as high potency flavoured hook-baits in conjunction with frozen ones as free offerings. It's always advisable that we remember to gas them with the same flavour added to the frozen maggots.

First take an empty 35mm-film case or similar container and remove the top. Now add just enough flavour to cover the bottom of the case (approx. 1.ml) and then add live maggots until three-quarters full. Now replace the top of the container securely and leave them in a cool dark place (Do not freeze) for a minimum of 24 hours; 48 is even better, as the added time will soften the maggots even further. Use them in large bunches of 15 to 20 straight hooked on a size 8 or 6, T-6 Raptor.

THE BIG BAIT METHOD

I am a firm believer that on many occasions a Big Barbel prefers to inspect (test) a static bait, and depending on what the bait is, will often nudge, mouth and ignore it before eventually having it. This is the principle upon which most of my fishing is based for I believe that even in warm, sunny, clear water daytime conditions, a large and well presented lump of meat will often prove difficult for the biggest fish to resist. It remains without doubt however that big baits are most effective in coloured water daytime conditions and from dusk into darkness regardless of water clarity.

Purely from a view of overall consistency, the big bait method still remains the most Big Barbel selective method we are likely to use – particularly whilst fishing blindly. It provides us with the opportunity to place a single hook-bait amongst a group of mixed sized Barbel, while at the same time offering us virtual assurance that once a proper bite arrives, it is most likely to be from a larger member of the group. The principle behind it is that the size of our hook-bait is such that the mouth of a specimen-sized fish only can negotiate it, and to a high degree the method is extremely successful.

Nevertheless, our Big Barbel successes never come guaranteed and so the method is by no means a certainty. Should a small Barbel manage to grip the bait by shall we say, grabbing hold of a corner, this will often result in a chunk being removed as the fish manages to bite cleanly through it. When rod topping or quiver tipping, this type of bite usually results in the rod tip being pulled only part way around before suddenly springing back. When touch legering, two to three inches of line will be drawn from the loop before all goes slack. If we retrieve the bait at this stage, we are likely to see that a perfectly formed semi-circular piece has been removed in the shape of a smaller Barbel's top lip.

Under these circumstances, I would recommend leaving the bait in position for a few more minutes as a proper bite could possibly develop. If however a similar sort of response follows and the bait is again dropped, I would advise retrieval and renewal of the hook-bait. Once this scenario begins to occur, it is highly probable that should the bait be left in position, it will merely be dwindled down to a size that fits adequately into that particular Barbel's mouth. Depending on both the size of the culprit and the bait we began with, this type of bite can last for a duration well in excess of 30 minutes; often resulting in a far smaller Barbel than we would have preferred. Lucky for us, though, is that by far the majority of fish captured on this method are of specimen size.

Our confidence in the method is probably far better gained if we begin by cutting a 300.gm tin of meat into 6 equal in size pieces. Once we begin to realise just how much a large Barbel can actually fit into its mouth, we should then feel confident enough to increase the bait size further by cutting the 300.gm block into only 3 pieces. (See how to cut and hook)

Whilst fishing this method we have all the usual options of bite detection open to us. Should we prefer to employ the more straightforward form of rod top legering, I would advise that once the initial knocks on the rod tip are detected and the bite begins to develop, we then give the fish a little line by lifting the butt section and dropping the tip towards the water before striking firmly.

The best ways to execute the method are to either touch-leger (as previously described), or to set the rod in two rests as low as the current strength of the river will allow. The rod should be positioned pointing towards the bait (with the bait-runner set at a little more than is needed for the current speed to take line) and the free-spool mechanism engaged. By watching the rod tip for the usual give-away knocks, we can then prepare ourselves for the spool to spin; then pick up the rod, turn the reel handle and strike firmly.

We should also note that while this method may increase our chances of capturing a Big Barbel, it also increases our chances of capturing nothing, particularly in those areas in which specimens are vastly outnumbered with smaller Barbel. We should not however allow this to dissuade us, for in these circumstances a proper bite may well take a while to arrive, but when it does eventually occur we had better hang on to that rod!

Brian Dowling. 10+ River Teme.

Steve Pope. River Severn 14.8

Steve Withers. Hampshire Avon 11+

The author. Trent Tributary 10lb 4.oz.

68.

THE ULTIMATE DESIGNER. From left to right. Hemp with fishmeal pellet. Meatball and designer base-mix. Pellet on top of 350gm tin denotes the scale!

Imitation caddis grub. A mealworm, or two!

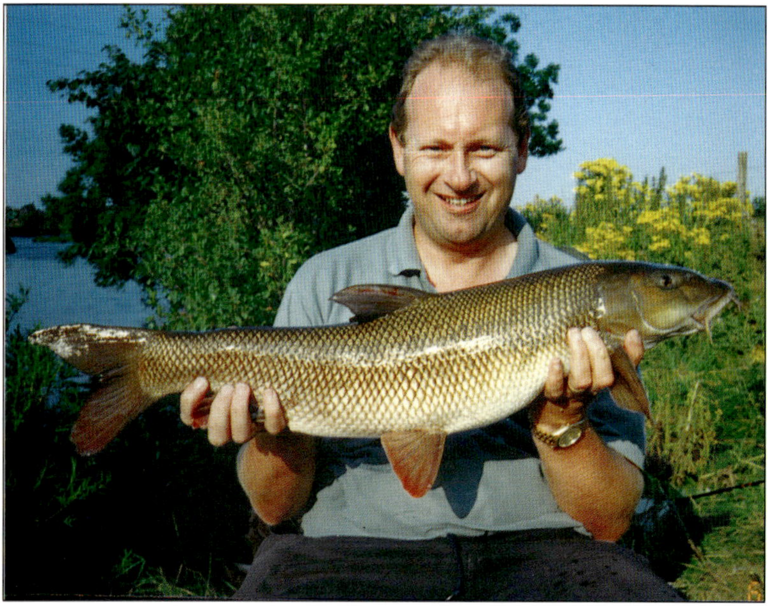

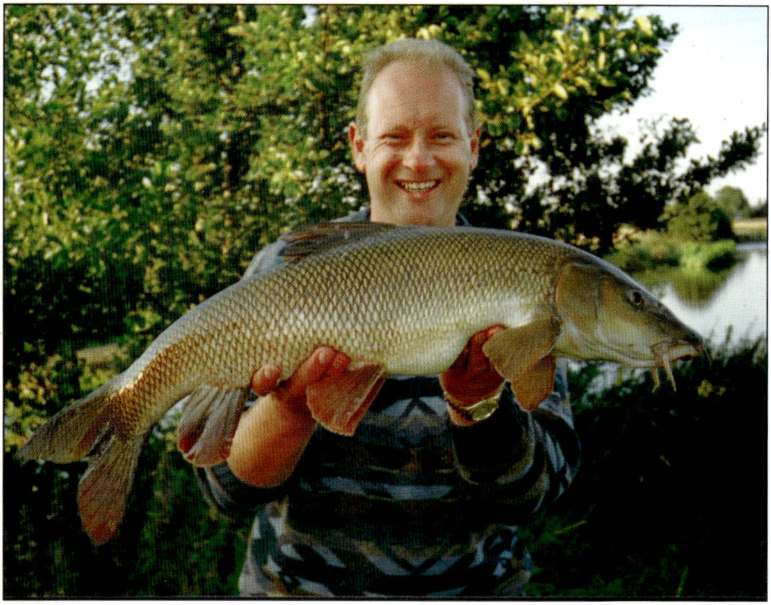

My own preferance for rod handle design comprises of fat, 35mm duplon grips both above and below the reel seat. This not only gives a feeling of total fish playing control, it also drastically reduces the symptoms of arm and elbow strain. Harrison Advanced Rods will fit these to special order, or will supply for your own custom rod building requirements.

Big Barbel love the protection of fallen trees. Providing of course that the bottom's right! See location.

One of the best touch legerer's in the business. Alex 'The Dentist' Young. 10.8 captured New Years Day 2000.

12.9 and author.

The unassuming Steve Withers and a 13.14 from the Dorset Stour.

Popped up corn straight off a 2" hooklink. Same rig can be used with a longer combi-link to vary the presentation.

Create elastic band feeder rig, also on page 108, like this.

Dead maggot stiff rig pictured can be just as effective with a suppler hooklink.

Slower water like this stretch of the Kennet often produces the biggest fish. Note how Bill Paxman has positioned his rods to point in the direction of the bait.

A Big female positions herself for spawning the natural way.

Approximately one and a half litres = around 35,000 Barbel eggs. See reproduction section.

Sunrise over the Hampshire Avon.

The original and magical sunset over the Dorset Stour. Taken and supplied by Steve Withers, and I'm sure most gratefully appreciated by us all!

CUTTING AND HOOKING BIG BAITS

1. Begin by chopping meat into six, equal in size, pieces.
Novice Big-Bait anglers should use the ones on the right. The more experienced may prefer those on the left. Shape and roughen the edges a little!

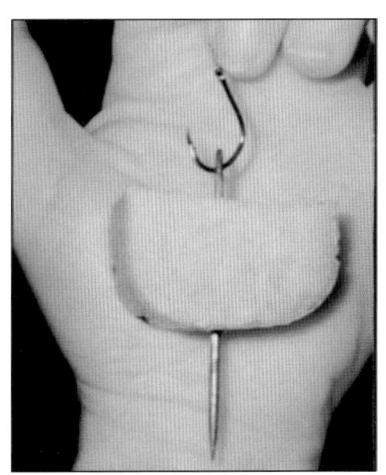

2. Pass baiting needle (bodkin) through the centre of the bait. Place the hook in the eye and pull the hook through as shown below.

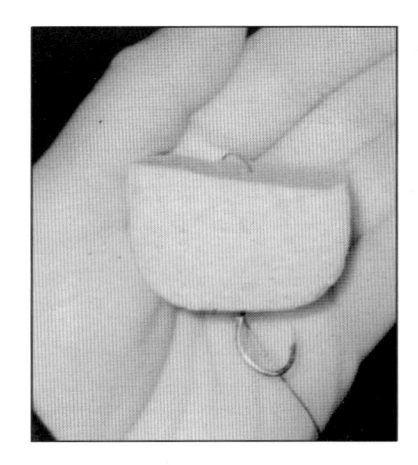

BIG BAITS.81

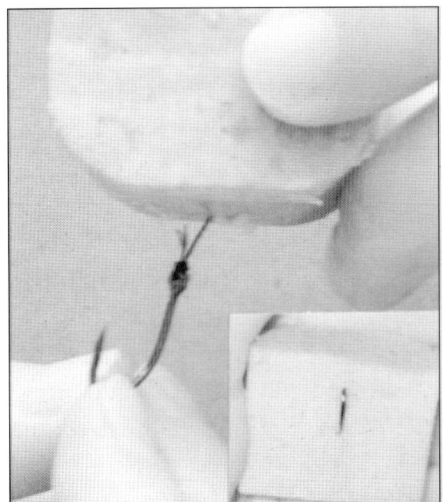

3. Once the hook is through, rotate and bury back inside the bait as shown.

Actual size below.

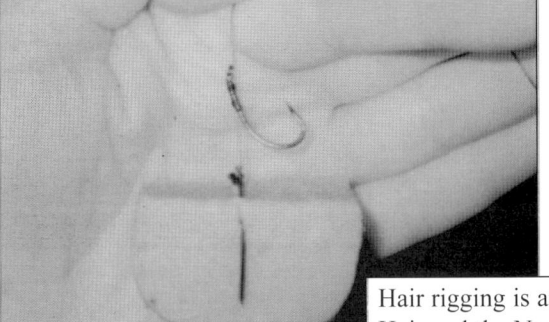

Hair rigging is an option. See the Hair and the Needle!

82.BIG BAITS

HAIR-RIGGING

THE HAIR AND THE NEEDLE

I'm sure each of us are aware of the conventional – through the middle – method of hair-rigging certain baits with a baiting needle. Whilst this remains a great method, its Achilles' heel is the cheese-wire effect that it has on a bait such as luncheon meat. If there is one thing that we are certain to encounter while using this method it is the attention of nuisance fish, which often detach a hair-rigged meat bait before a Big Barbel can have it. Once those annoying rod taps begin, the angler's mind often becomes invaded with doubts as to whether the bait is still attached; and more often than not, it isn't.

For a number of seasons, I have been using a hair with a difference. The presentation is the same where it matters (in the water) and it has significantly reduced many of the doubts associated with the conventional method. Once tied, we can be fishing a hair-rigged meat bait (or similar) with increased confidence and do not require a baiting needle to mount it. The principle behind it is to present the bait on a hair, but with the anchor going around it instead of through it. The example given employs the use of a number eight dark grey pole elastic (used because of its more than adequate stretch) and is best constructed as follows.

1. Take a long length of elastic and remove its oily coating by soaking and washing in warm soapy water; then dry it. (At this point you will know if the oil is fully removed. If it isn't, the elastic won't knot properly and will need further washing.)
2. Tie a loop (pound coin size) in the elastic and cut from the main piece.
3. Tie the elastic loop to the braided hook-length.
4. Position the top of the loop just below the bend of the hook and attach the hook-length using a knotless knot.
5. Attach the swivel using a palomar knot, and your basic hook-link is complete.

To mount a hook-bait simply open out the elastic, place in the bait and release the elastic when central. Finish off by scoring around the bait with a fingernail and the elastic will sink slightly into the bait. Simple, or what?

The trick is to get the size of the band to bait ratio correct. Once this is achieved, we have a hair-rigged bait which nuisance fish find extremely difficult to remove. Consequently, we have increased our chances of a Big Barbel eventually finding it.

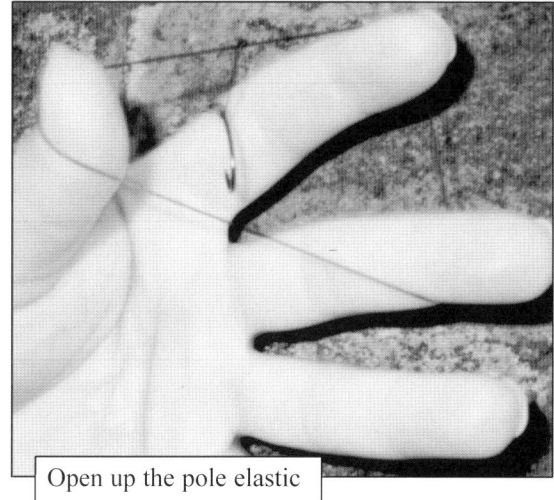

Open up the pole elastic

BAITS ON ELASTIC

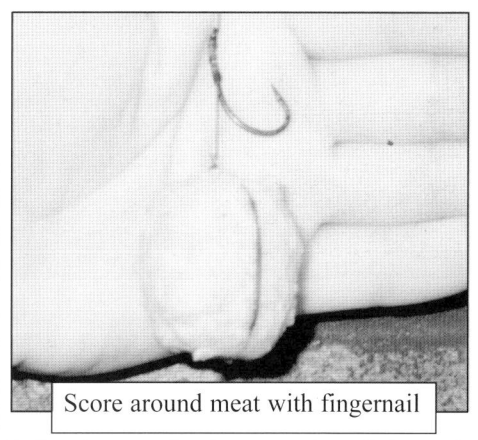

Along with most canned meats, high fat content (stiffly made) paste baits such as those made with cheese or sausage meat can also be used to great effect. Because of their lengthy resistance to hydro breakdown these pastes stay on the band for long periods. The larger of the increasingly popular fishmeal pellets can also be used with confidence. Experimentation is vital to achieve a personal balance and preferred bait size.

Score around meat with fingernail

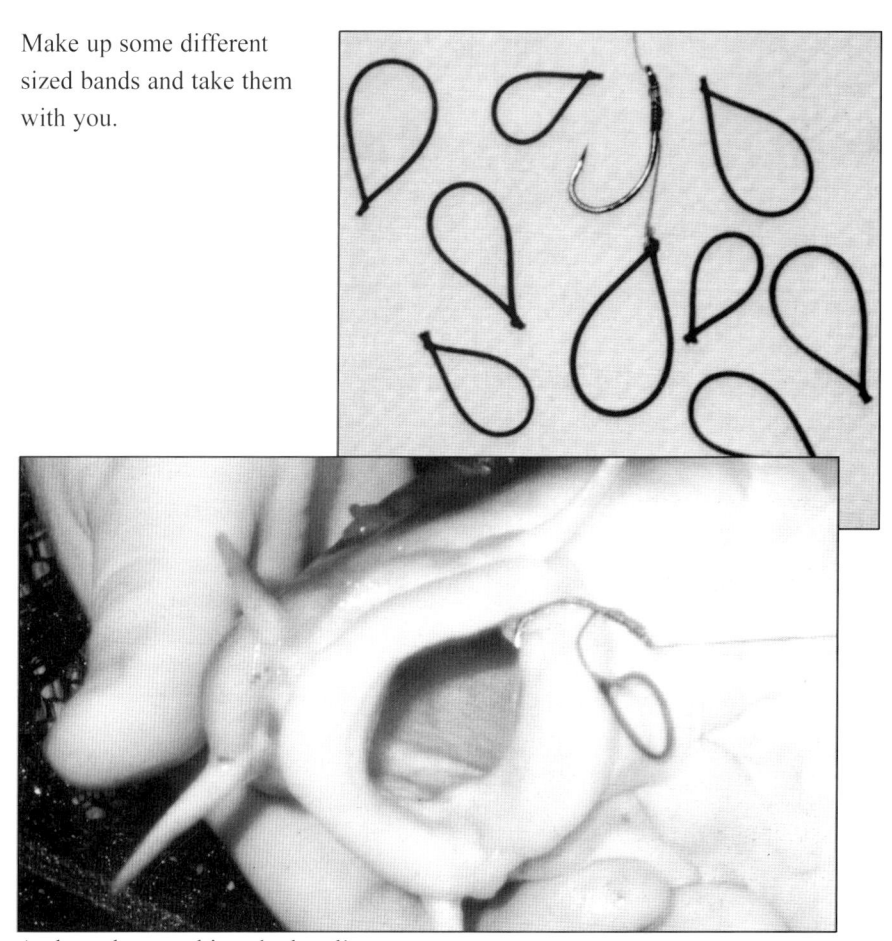

Make up some different sized bands and take them with you.

And another one bites the band!

HEMP BOMBS

In the event that we are fishing an extremely pressured stretch of river, sometimes the only thing that divides success from failure is to do something a little different from the norm. The norm on most of the over-fished venues is for many anglers to immediately deposit four or five pints of hemp into their swim upon arrival. While the Barbel pulling power of the hempseed's aroma is unquestionable, I share the belief of many anglers that pressured Big Barbel often refuse to feed over large quantities which suddenly appear on the riverbed.

An excellent way to maximise the effect of the seeds' aroma, without alarming the bigger fish too much, is to liquidise it and place it on the riverbed as inconspicuously as possible. This can be achieved far more simply by using what I call hemp bombs. To make half a dozen pear-size bombs (enough to bait three swims), I will liquidise one pint of hemp and mix it with a little brown crumb; adding a small amount of liquidised sweetcorn to help bind it.

The Bomb Factory

DANGER. UXB!

I then mould the stiffened mixture around, six, large three-inch raw-plugs with a loop of nylon tied to each of them and store them uncovered in the garage/shed over night to form a dry skin surface. When fishing a near bank swim with a steady flow, I attach the loop on the bomb to a clip swivel tied to the mainline and place the bomb on the riverbed a rod length out by opening the bale arm and releasing it to sink to the bottom. This creates only minimal swim disturbance as no cast is actually made.

I then leave it to rest for about thirty seconds; then lift the rod top to remove and retrieve the raw-plug. The centre of the bomb then floods with water and the breakdown process begins. Little more than

86.HEMP BOMBS

thirty minutes later there is a carpet of Barbel attracting hemp and corn particles right where I position my hook-bait. The bombs become even more attractive if the fish attack them, as they simply explode into hemp oil-laden clouds. No more than two bombs per swim should be introduced, as there is a risk of the fish becoming totally pre-occupied in searching for the tiny particles.

INTO THE WILDERNESS

One of the most satisfying ways in which to capture specimen Barbel is for us to venture into the wilderness – those untamed stretches of our particular river where very few, if indeed any anglers at all, have been before us. There is something that will always remain eternally magical about capturing a beautiful Big Barbel that has quite possibly never felt the tempered steel of a sharp hook before. While such areas are not as uncommon to many rivers as we may think, access to them is possibly not too convenient and is likely to both involve a considerably long walk and a certain degree of manual labour (in the form of swim-cutting) for the pioneer.

Those amongst us who wish to consider such an approach will be highly unlikely to need me to tell them that tackle should be kept to a bare minimum. (An angler's waistcoat always remains a good investment under these circumstances.) What many anglers may fail to consider, however, is the degree of importance to which they should give to the bait they will carry. After all, the isolated Barbel population is highly unlikely to respond to any bait at all that is non-natural; with the only exception likely to be cheese.

For some strange reason (see my theory in Scents and 'Scentsability'), cheese remains the most instantly effective of the non-natural baits to date, and for that reason alone is always worth a try. The only other sensible option open to us initially is to use natural baits such as lobworms and/or minnows. When caddis are in season, it may well prove worth our while to take along a few mealworms also. Once we have located a few specimen size fish, by either sight or capturing them, we always have the option to return to the area on a regular basis. We can then, surprisingly quite rapidly, wean them onto the likes of meat-baits and fish in a far more selective manner – especially in those areas where the fish cannot be too easily seen and located.

We should also consider that because the Barbel will be uneducated towards our methods and terminal rigs, it is highly unlikely that we will require the assistance of a hair-rig. It remains crucial that should we wish to spend a few weeks, or even months, familiarising ourselves with what could well be described as Barbel Heaven, any refinements within our presentation are left for as long a period as possible; and made only according to the Barbels' response.

THE THREE-SWIM ROTATION SYSTEM

Whether we are pioneering or quite simply fishing a more popular stretch blindly, the three-swim rotation system can offer us a speedy way of Big Barbel location. The simple idea behind this method is to pick out what appears to be three potential swims; keep them consistently, though not too heavily baited and fish them in rotation, making certain that each is fished into prime time (darkness) on a minimum of two occasions. The half a dozen sessions required to do this can be fished either consecutively (as those of us with plenty of time on our hands may prefer) or staggered. In the case that sessions are to be staggered, I would advise a period of no more than 24 hours be allowed to pass between each. The method can be successful when a rest period of 48 hours is allowed, but the larger the time-span between each session the less effective the method obviously becomes.

The best way to employ this system is for us to pick out the big fish potential of each of our three chosen swims. If each swim were thought of as being equally potential to the other, that would be ideal. However, it is more likely that our sixth sense, or gut instincts, will point us in the direction of a preference for either swim one, two or three. For this example, let us imagine that it is dark by 9.00pm. No-1 swim is where we suspect a true monster to be. No-2 is our second favourite and No-3 we are not too sure about. The nearer each swim is to the other, the better for us it will be. We arrive at 6.00pm and immediately introduce a few free food offerings into swims 1 and 2. Allowing for 30 minutes to both set up and bait up; we begin to fish swim 3 at 6.30pm; having introduced nothing prior to the hook-bait.

Our intention is to fish for a minimum of one hour in each swim. Having had nothing in swim 3 by 7.30pm we then introduce a few free offerings before leaving. We then move to swim 2 and introduce a hook-bait only. We may even take a good fish from swim 2 and be tempted to ignore swim 1 completely. This of course remains our option, but if we are to carry out our plan we must stick to the rules, and can take great satisfaction from knowing we can probably rely on swim 2 in the future. In any event, on a smaller river that is only slightly pressured, I would always recommend giving a swim that has just produced a fish a rest period. Our idea should now be to sit it out in swim 1 from 8.30 until 9.30pm, even later if possible.

Whether our first session has been a success or not isn't really that crucial. What is important is that we have begun our little campaign, and now have at least five more sessions to cover the same three swims in a different sequence, conditions permitting of course. It's always a good idea to introduce a few more free bait samples into each swim as we leave. When using this method, we should always prepare ourselves for the unexpected; as it's just possible that the least fancied swim of all could well be the one that finally produces. Also, whenever circumstances allow, I recommend that more than two periods are allowed for each swim, particularly whilst pioneering untouched areas where a lengthier programme of non-natural bait introduction will need to be considered. Just remember to take some cheese along to the more remote areas for a little instant non-natural success, but don't ever forget that those nuisance chub also like it!

KNOT TYING

THE PALOMAR

1. Pass line back on itself to Form a loop.

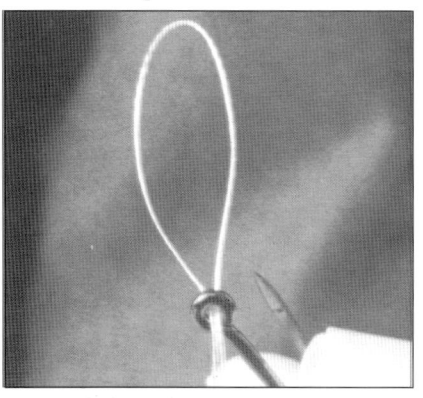

2. Double loop over and pass back through itself.

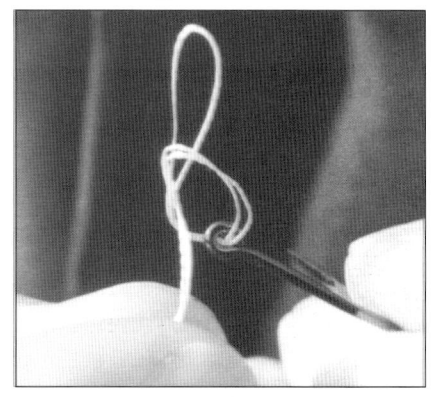

3. Take the 'pass-through' loop and pass over the hook or swivel.

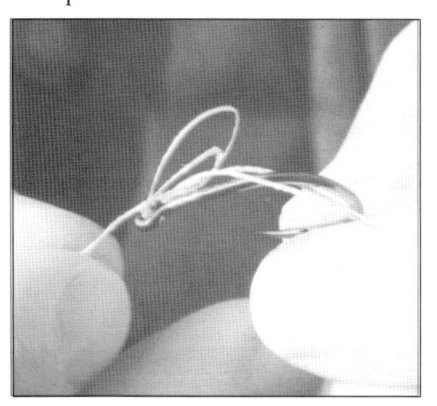

4. Wet the line and draw the loop steadily into a knot.

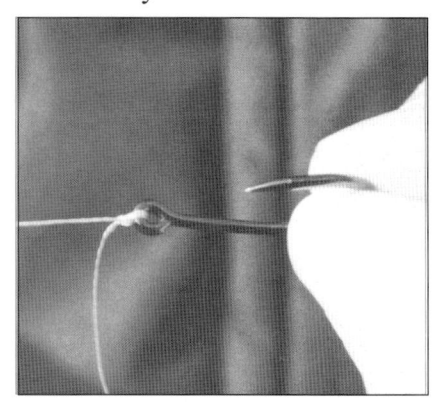

THE KNOT-LESS KNOT

1. Whilst holding one end of the line tight to the hook-shank, pass the other loose end through eye.

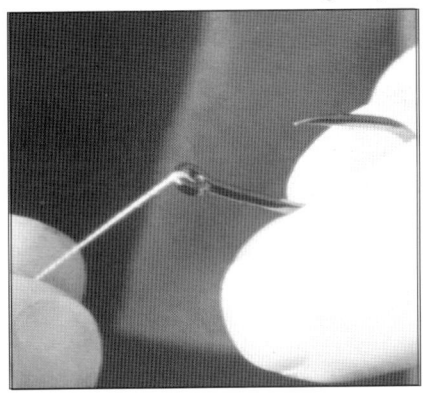

2. Starting from the top, wrap line back down the shank for approx. 9 – 12 turns.

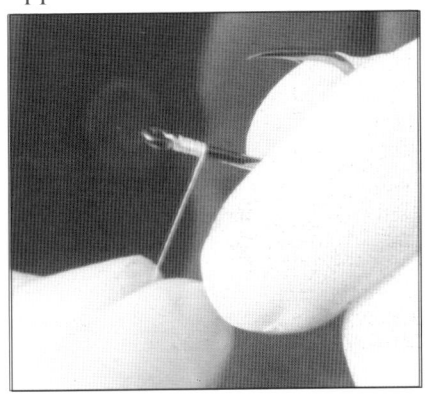

3. Pass the line through the eye once again.

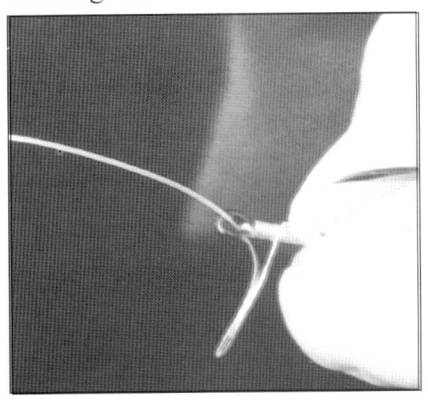

4. Draw the knot up to complete.

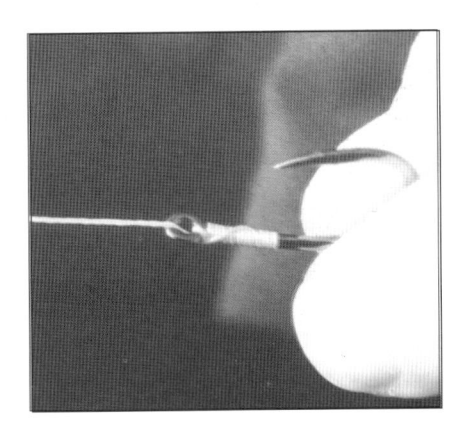

THE MAHSEER KNOT

1. Form a loop by passing line twice through the eye in the same direction.

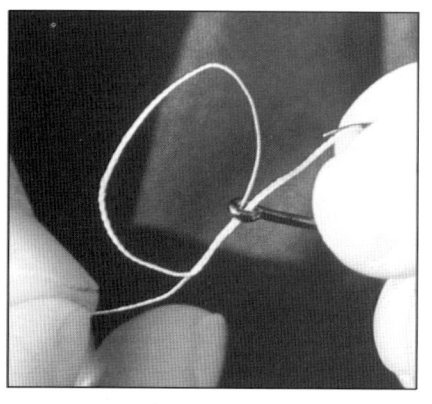

2. Take loose end and wrap around the mainline 4 to 5 times.

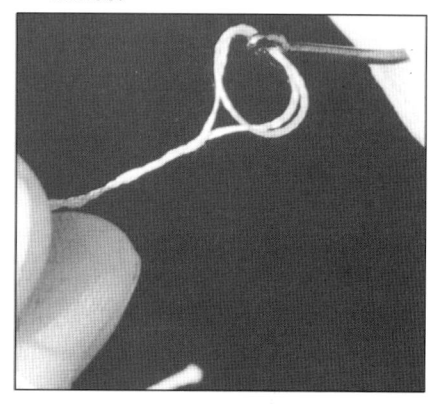

3. Pass the tag-end back through the double loop.

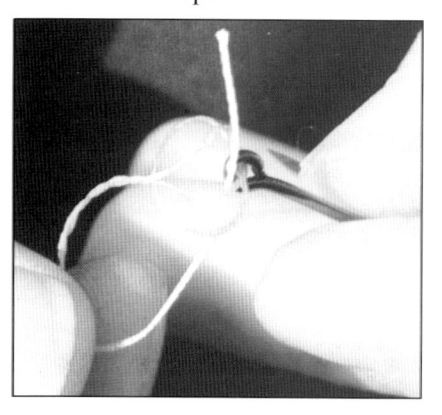

4. Wet the line, draw the knot and trim.

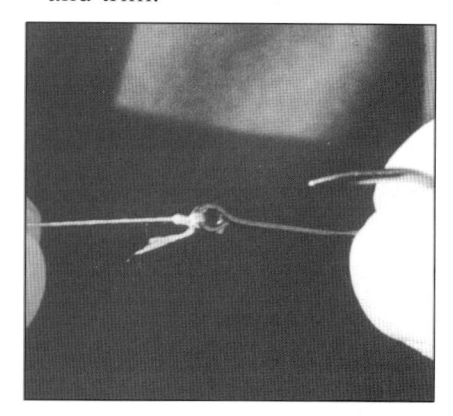

Note! If the double loop of the palomar or mahseer is crossed over instead of parallel when the knot is tightened, the line will cut back into itself and so will break at less than half the stated mainline breaking strain. Check it before it's too late!

HOOKLENGTHS AND RIGS

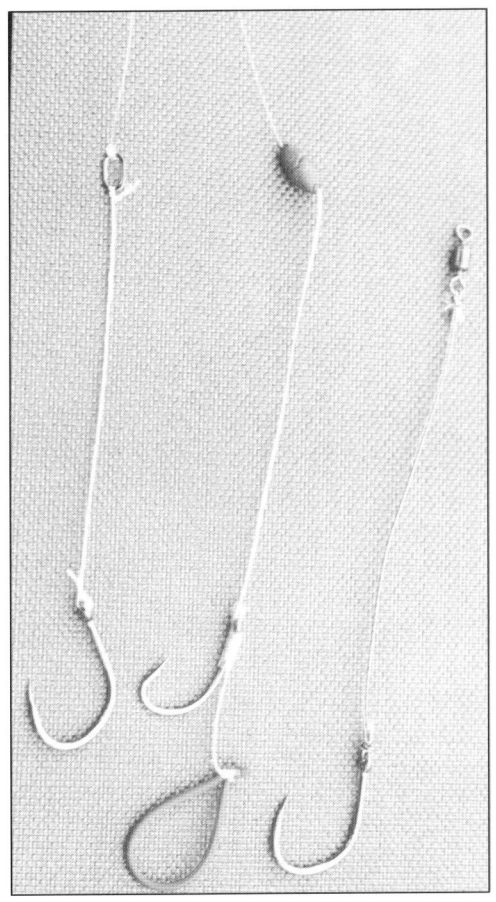

Create fluorocarbon and braid combi-links by using ESP oval rings or size 11 swivels.

In clear-water, daytime conditions, no more than the final two inches should be braid.

Apply Kryston drop-em to oval ring to pin the link to the riverbed.

When using swivels, apply drop-em only to the above fluorocarbon knot to ease line twist.

Depending on the type of swim, we intend fishing, daytime combi-links may vary from 2 to 5 feet in length.

A few different weights to hold bottom with.

For additional tips, see leger stops and backleads on page 109.

A selection of hooklength materials. Reverge or Sightfree offer a less visible presentation with combi-links. Use Ghost for creating stiff rigs with fluorocarbon straight to an Owner SSW hook that matches the bait size. 12lb Double T Synthesis or Kryston 14lb super-silk are both good pop-up materials – especially with sweetcorn. Always use a uni-link swivel for any stiff or pop-up rig as they offer a hinged effect to the hooklength!

A little bit of Araldite, some pebbles, mono, a bit of black ink and a little time, and we can create 'spook-free' weights just like these.

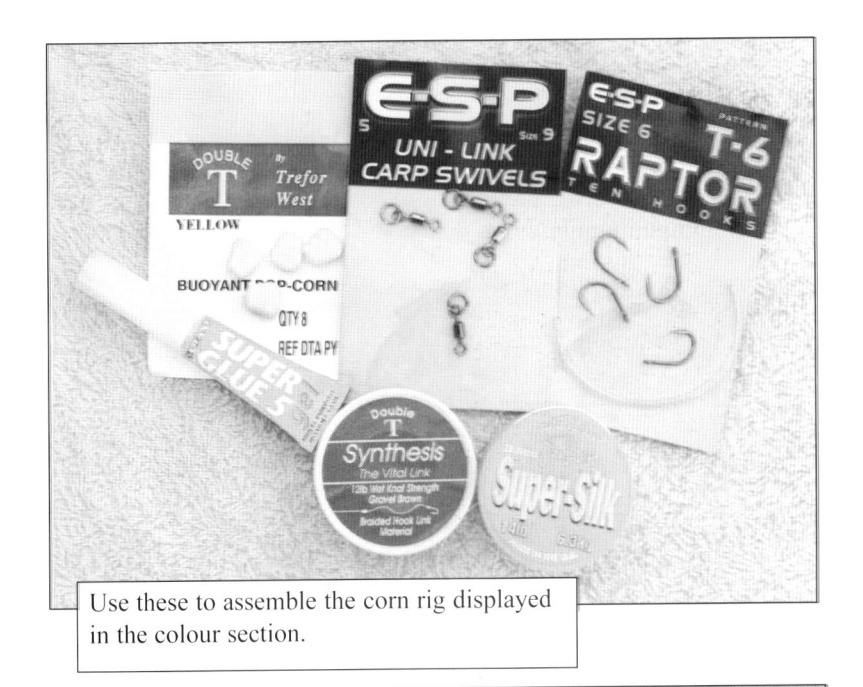

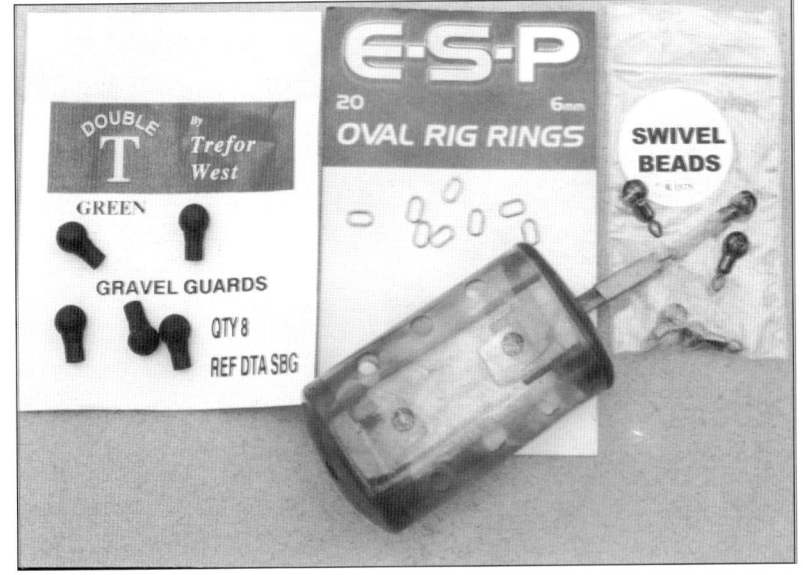

Use these to assemble the corn rig displayed in the colour section.

When using any feeder that is fitted with a standard type swivel, always change it to a swivel bead. See colour section for rig.

RIGS.95

Mealworms can be hooked as shown here – three up on a size 8 T-6 Raptor, or six/eight up on a size 6.

Hair rigging mealworms only becomes necessary for pressured fish. This can be done by gluing them back to back with hair between.

As with corn or any other superglue hair rig, the gel type is easier and safer to apply than the runny type! Casters can be set up in the same way.

Hairgrip weights. Create pop-up weights by using a length of stiff rig tubing. The swivel housing is made by pushing a small piece of silicon tube over both ends before wrapping around the clay!

96.RIGS

A selection
of bait-droppers.

The practical Double T unhooking mat 'doubles' up as a cushioned seat and is ideal for the roving anglers amongst us. The rig-keeper wallet also comes in handy for carrying a number of ready tied hook-lengths. See useful addresses for enquiries on all Double T products.

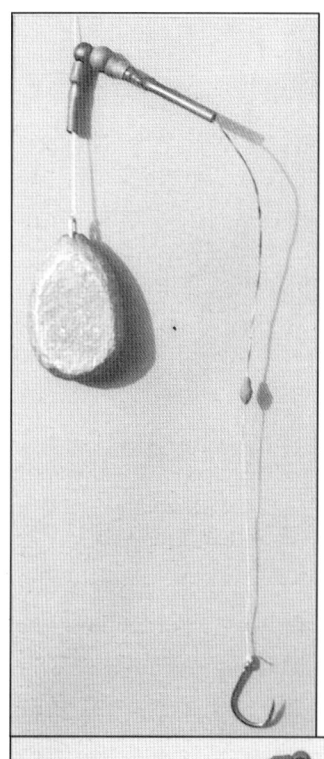

This is a highly effective rig when used in high and coloured water. It has the added safety of a home-made, breakaway powergum link.

The link is simplicity itself, and its disclosure is dedicated to the memory of the late, Gordon Scott, who first publicised its construction in the Barbel Society internal magazine, Barbel Fisher.

1. Slide a swivel bead on 7lb powergum and tie with a single overhand knot, creating a 2in (50mm) loop. The longer the leads used the longer the loop.
2. Move the knot round to the swivel eye and slide a small piece of silicon tube over knot and eye.
3. When in use, push the loop through the leger swivel and the leger through the loop.
4. To detach for quick change purposes reverse the process. Simple but highly effective.

To make my 10/12in hook-link.

1. Take a length of 15lb Snakebite and remove half of the coating.
2. Tie a swivel to the coated end and slide a 1-2in piece of silicon onto the line before tying on the hook.
3. When in use, attach to mainline fitted with a Double T gravel bead and a second round bead (optional) and slide silicon tube over swivel to form anti-tangle effect.

98.RIGS

ROUTINE MAINTENANCE

Even accounting for the well documented theories regarding nomadic specimens, there's increasing evidence through the consistency of recaptures which suggests a higher proportion of the Big Barbel population within many of our rivers is extremely territorial. Many specialist anglers of course already suspect this, and the best possible example can again be taken from that particular stretch of the Great Ouse, where many big fish anglers return in their pursuit of known individual specimens. This practice is also carried out on many other Barbel rivers throughout the whole country, but because these Barbel are likely to be a little smaller (even though they are still an admirable catch), they sadly appear not to generate the same interest and appeal as the Ouse monsters.

One particularly important point to note is that regardless of whether a Barbel is nine or nineteen pounds; they are all creatures of habit. Every single Barbel that is residential to any one particular area will know every square inch and contour of the riverbed around which it lives, inside out. Each individual at sometime or other will have explored every nook and cranny as they seek out any newly formed feeding areas. However, as interesting as this may appear, it is not the new but rather the older, more established habitual food seeking routines of the bigger fish that we are concerned with; for it is these we can most definitely exploit with the assistance of a little routine maintenance.

Each large individual group member will have formed a set pattern of routine for feeding. Although these feeding times will remain open to fluctuation in a swim that has not been pre-baited, each individual fish will set out in its search for food in a pre-determined direction and follow a pre-determined route. In some instances, the same route will be temporarily shared by more than one fish, but at some point they will become divided and take to their own path. As in sight selection, we can only observe these routes through gin-clear water. But, unlike the mass bait induced feeding described within sight selection, we need only introduce a small quantity of free offerings as our success rests entirely upon our knowledge of the target fish's pattern of routine. The method of routine maintenance, while extremely effective, requires far more of our patience, perseverance and time, than any other method described in this book, as it can sometimes take days rather than hours of observation before we can effectively position a hook-bait. Do not be put off by this, especially when chasing monstrous fish, or perhaps even a national record. Plotting the downfall of any big Barbel is often as exciting as capturing it.

This example involves the hypothetical movements of two Big Barbel. One just happens to be far bigger that the other. Using our most stealthy approach, we begin to observe the habits of both fish. (This is always far easier to do when we can safely climb nearby trees, or structures of any kind.) We now observe both specimens vacating the area from which we spotted them (usually, but not always, close to a snag of some kind) travelling in the direction towards the near bank. One fish remains closely behind the other for a distance of 15 metres before their paths become divided. We can now concentrate totally on the movements of the bigger fish and save the scalp of the smaller (although still big) specimen for a future date.

Although we have been observing the Big Barbel's movements for only a short period of time, even at such an early stage, it should immediately become obvious to us that the fish is moving in a very methodical fashion. In all probability, the fish is likely to be following a well-travelled channel (or trail) in the riverbed that may be little more than a few inches wide and possibly no more than 1 to 2 inches deeper than other contours within the bottom. The fish will undoubtedly make use of the same readily available channels that enable it to visit areas extremely close to the bank. Once we have built up a clear and concise picture of these navigable channels, we can then begin to introduce free food samples along our most conveniently accessible ones. (The closer to the bank the better.) It's crucial that any such free offerings are positioned accurately within the channel, as this will virtually guarantee a pick-up.

Providing we avoid using any food items that are likely to alarm pressured fish, any accurately positioned free offerings are likely to be consumed without the slightest hesitation, while those that have strayed only slightly off track are likely to be ignored completely. Once we have witnessed these free offerings being readily accepted, we can return to the area on a different occasion, observe the fish as it again begins its habitual cycle, and carefully position a hook-bait only minutes before the fish is due to arrive. Because of the possible lengthy time scale involved with this method, I recommend that we occasionally return to areas and methods we are more familiar and confident with, especially when any such area is nearby. That way our session can become divided between the two areas. This will greatly assist those of us who may well be tempted to ruin the effects of this method by presenting a hook-bait pre-maturely.

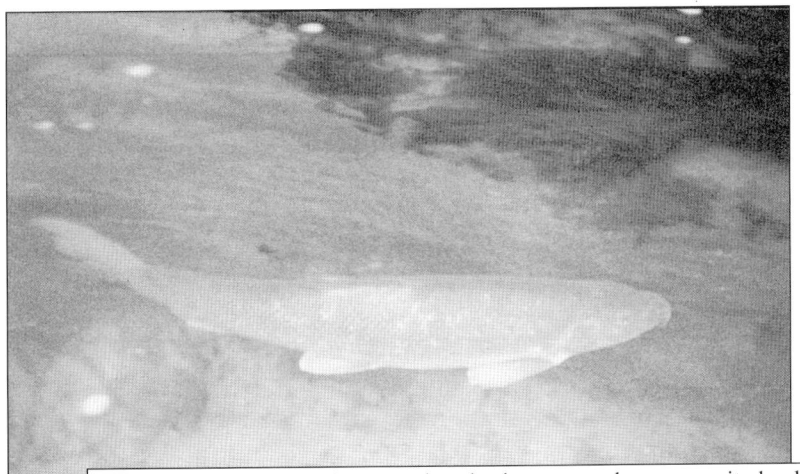

Anear double patrols in water barely deep enough to cover its back

By observing the fishes behaviour through the clear and warmer waters of the summer, we are then able to use our accumulated knowledge of each Big Barbel's habits to assist us in the hours of darkness and through the more coloured water conditions of the autumn and winter. A point to note is that once temperatures begin to fall along with the metabolic rate of the fish, each feeding spell will last for a shorter duration. Although the fish will leave the swim in the same direction (providing the swim is an annual one), the route each individual Barbel takes is also likely to cover a far shorter distance. It is therefore a good idea to place our hook-bait in the nearest possible channel to where the fish themselves reside.

Howard Maddocks with his brolly, and that magnificent Severn 16.3.

THE ULTIMATE BIG BARBEL EXPERIENCE
(A GUIDE TO BITES, HOOKING AND PLAYING BIG BARBEL AROUND SNAGS)

These days, most of my fishing involves the hit and hold approach with the bend of the rod being all that a hooked Barbel is allowed to have. This type of angling offers the most exciting sport that we could possibly wish for, and if you haven't yet experienced it yourselves then I seriously recommend that you try it. It's heart-stopping, lip-smacking, gut-busting, knee-trembling, arm-aching action. It is quite simply The Ultimate Big Barbel Experience!

Bites while snag-swim fishing will usually range from strong, confident pulls to rip the rod in wrenches. If this is the case, then we must make hay while the sun shines because this is a sign that the fish are not unduly pressured and may even be tempted from their cover during the day. More often than not, however, we are likely to be faced with the problem of following the kamikaze angler who hooks them all and never sees any of them. In this instance, bites may be nothing more than a virtually unhittable, short, sharp bang on the rod top. In these daytime situations I would advise the use of a long fluorocarbon hook-link (see hook-length assembly and rigs) that is anything from 3 to 5 feet in length. We then need to position the bait tight to the snag, and once in position must resist all temptation to move it. A proper bite will usually follow a patient wait of anything up to an hour or so. Any persistent finicky bites will be far better detected by those of us who touch-leger.

Once our Big Barbel is hooked it will become extremely angry, and providing that we survive the first thirty seconds, we should have an indication of who will win the battle. And a battle it is! Hit and hold Big Barbel fishing is not for the faint hearted. It is often one huge adrenaline rush that leaves us either trembling with excitement or shaking (and quite possibly swearing) in disappointment. Much of it depends on how we react after the bite arrives, and whether or not the hook is properly home.

10.12

The first fundamental mistake that we can make is not to strike. The times I have heard that, because Barbel often bite so fiercely, there is no need to strike. Granted, there is no need to jolt the rod as if setting the hook at distance, but a short and firm pull against the bite never did a good hook-hold any arm at all.

Another basis for error is to lift the rod in a skyward direction. Doing this gives the Barbel total control from the moment it is hooked. All it needs to do is open out its pectoral fins, let the force of the water push over its back, and it can then kite in whichever direction it so chooses. There is very little we can do with the rod in this position because we don't have the leverage to do it with. The harder we pull upwards the harder the Barbel will pull downwards. And the steeper the angle of line running through the water to the rod tip, the more chance there is of it being rubbed against a snag until a breakage occurs.

The secret of getting Big Barbel under control is to unbalance them as quickly as possible. To do this I will immediately drop the rod tip towards the water, thereby reducing the angle of line to the rod top and the fish's mouth. After about 10 to 15 seconds of me hanging on for life while letting the rod absorb the initial pressure by pulling only slightly in the opposite direction, the fish will begin to rise in the water. Once their stomach is no longer hugging the bottom, they become off balance and are far easier to control.

Initially, I always cup my free hand over the reel spool to stop it giving line until the fish is safely away from the snag, where it can then be played out in the normal way. Should it decide to head back in the direction of the snag, then side strain with a low rod is once again applied until control is fully re-established. The anti-reverse is also engaged with a stiffly set clutch throughout the whole duration of the fight. A good point always worth remembering is that a hooked and angry Barbel will, under most circumstances, pull in the exact opposite direction to that in which it is being pulled. I appreciate that it may all sound a little difficult, but it does come fairly easily with practice. Try it and see!

DEMORALISATION

No matter how many Big Barbel captures we are fortunate enough to enjoy, there will always remain those sessions throughout the duration of any one season when we wonder why the hell we go fishing at all. We should savour our successes when they arrive and must learn never to take them for granted: for in the world of specimen Barbel angling, we seldom experience so much exciting pleasure without having to endure a certain degree of pain.

It's really quite amazing how the confidence that comes through a string of successful captures vanishes almost completely once a few blank sessions are strung together. In all probability, we each have our very own individual levels of tolerance towards a successive run of bad luck, but once our confidence becomes only even slightly dented, the symptoms of demoralisation will begin to develop. To blank half a dozen times in a row in conditions that are supposed to be text-book perfect is enough to give anyone a dose of blank affective demoralisation (or B.A.D for short). The first classic symptom to appear is that a systematic invasion of doubts flood into our minds as we begin to question our whole tactical approach. Victims of such misfortune have been known to suffer temporary bouts of a kind of madness that sees them consider selling their tackle. In extreme cases, some individuals even consider taking up carp fishing although, thankfully, this is only very rare.

In all seriousness, though, it's important that we do not end up in the very common position of feeling too deflated by such an unfortunate run of events. It is extremely easy to fall into the trap of letting our heads go down, and it's common for this sad and sorry symptom to occur even before we make our way to the river. Depending totally upon the degree as to which B.A.D effects us individually, some of us really do become tempted to throw in the towel and call it a day. Yes; if we allow it; it really can become that bad!

The worst thing about this whole scenario is that if we do nothing to improve it, it very often gets worse before it gets better. As so much of our success is dependent on our levels of confidence, once this is dented we become less effective big fish anglers. We often develop a lack of patience. We uncharacteristically fidget whilst waiting for a bite; we retrieve hook-baits prematurely. We are consistently wondering why the hell it's all gone pear-shaped; whether the fish are still there; whether the bait is still intact; whether we are tangled or have hooked up with the bottom; whether the rig's right, etc, etc…

In these situations even the hardiest, well-seasoned, specimen angler will struggle to remain focussed, but for anyone who is relatively new to the wonderful game of big fish angling I think a change may well prove to be as good as a rest. Many of us who once regularly fished for Barbel of any size still have our basic angling skills to fall back on, and there is often nothing more refreshingly basic and fun than some good old Barbel bashing with a swim-feeder. As far as the waning confidence of the specimen Barbel angler is concerned, a couple of sessions on the maggot-feeder could be just what the good doctor ordered.

RETURNING TO BASICS

Obviously we improve our own chances of a successful return to basics by ensuring that we again visit areas that have produced many average sized Barbel for us in the past. As the whole object of this exercise is to restore enough of our dented confidence to return to the often slower producing areas of our Big Barbel hunting, we must be as sure as we possibly can be that we are about to place our swim-feeder among some fish.

In the unfortunate circumstances that swim-feeder tactics are over-used in such an area, it is often a good tactic to fish for the first hour or so without a hook-link attached. Even smaller barbel become educated to the ways of angling and very often require a little coaxing, and an hour's worth of problem-free feeding can promote so much confidence within the entire shoal that they may well begin to attack the feeder as it enters the swim. Should we not be able to clearly see this happening through the water, we will only need to observe the rod tip as it dances and jumps back and forth until the feeder becomes empty.

This kind of rod-twitching activity is easily distinguishable from the tapping attentions of the smaller dace, minnows and such like, as it's quite common for the odd Barbel to take the feeder partially into its mouth, pulling the rod top around almost as a proper bite would be indicated. Once this activity begins to occur, we should let it continue for as long as our temptation will allow before attaching a hook-link, as the more members of the shoal become confident the more of them we are likely to catch.

It is often possible to induce feeding activity by introducing a half to one pint of bait as quickly as possible. Whilst fishing a far bank swim, precision accurate and consecutively repeated casts should be made until the desired amount of bait has been introduced. On occasions this disturbance will temporarily see the shoal vacate the swim, but it is far more likely that our activity will be tolerated and a response made rather rapidly. Once our initial bait introduction has been made, we should then be thinking of casting our hook-link free feeder at three-minute intervals. It is important that a consistent flow of food is maintained and three minutes gives us sufficient time to observe the rod tip for any tell tale signs of activity. Once this has begun, it is then in our interest to lengthen the intervals between casting to four and then five minutes, as this will keep the fish working over the area of bait distribution. We should of course remain aware that such a positive reaction will not always be forthcoming, but on the occasions it is, it's common for us to begin catching immediately upon casting a baited hook.

During those occasions that the Barbel respond more slowly, it is likely this feeder knocking activity will begin further into the session – after the hook-length has been attached for some time. Once such activity begins, it's common practice for the angler to begin striking at what first appears to be rod-bending bites. However, once a strike is met with no resistance and a retrieval of the terminal rig made, it is not unusual for the hook-bait to appear totally untouched.

I first encountered this extremely common scenario on the highly pressured match fished sections of the middle Severn. It's almost habitual for these extremely pressured fish to ignore the hook-bait completely and feed only on the maggots that escape from the holes of the feeder. A trick that I regularly used to employ in the early 90s was the elastic band rig. Instead of using the more conventional hook-link size of 16 to 20 inches, a far shorter length of only 6 inches is used. The idea behind this method is to attach a wide elastic band to the body of the feeder and use it to trap the hook close to an escape hole, thereby mimicking naturally escaping maggots.

Used in the circumstances described, the method is devastatingly effective in taking multiple numbers of unsuspecting shoal fish. As the Barbel will have gained the necessary confidence to begin attacking the feeder, as soon as we become aware of their presence we can change to the method as soon as we like. I should warn the unsuspecting amongst us that within seconds of making the change to this rig, those 'ghost' bites are likely to become very real and we should prepare ourselves for some rather hectic action.

The methods described here work far more effectively throughout the summer and autumn, and I would expect to use a minimum of three to four pints of live maggots within a five-hour session. It is always worth experimenting with flavours to assist a more rapid and prolonged response – and we mustn't forget to try a few chopped maggots. I would also recommend that, whenever possible, we make

The elastic band feeder rig. Even when fishing for medium sized Barbel, there is always the possibility that a big fish will show. Be prepared at all times. A fairly supple presentation can be achieved by using Trilene XL as a hook-link. Fluorocarbon offers a stiffer but practically invisible alternative. Always use 10lb breaking strain lines as a first choice for all forms of Barbel feeder fishing. Never drop below 8lb breaking strain when using smaller hooks. A reliable pattern of hook for a slightly finer presentation is the Gold Label, SS penetrator. Although for photographic purposes I have used a size 10 T-6 Raptor and three maggots, the SS in the same size has a slightly smaller gape and appears more suitable for presenting double maggot. A clearer picture of the rig construction can be seen in the colour section.

Bill Paxman. River Kennet. 12.15

LEGER STOPS AND BACKLEADS

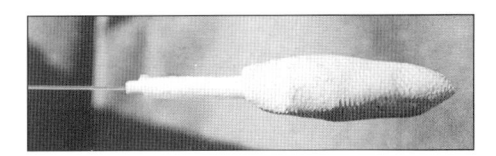

When faced with the problems of fishing in gin clear water, we often need to consider the use of a backlead. This will sink the line a few feet behind our terminal rig and may further encourage pressured fish to pick up our bait. Although I will occasionally use a leadcore line such as, kryston Score, I prefer to attach a piece of cocktail stick to the line with silicon tube as shown here. Plasticene is then applied over the entire half-inch length and I have a sliding backlead that I can move at will. By cutting the stick and tube to one and a half inch and leaving off the plasticene, a sturdy, line friendly and adjustable leger stop can be created for rigs that require that the mainline goes closer, or even straight through to the hook. (Clear tube used to show example. Use green or black when assembling.)

TACTICS

AUTUMN AND WINTER

WATER TEMPERATURE
UNDER PRESSURE
BEWARE THE CRYSTAL BALL
BAIT SIZE AND QUANTITY
GRID FISHING
FISHING IN THE DARK

The relatively recent and much wider understanding of their behaviour is now encouraging more specimen anglers to pursue the species throughout the winter. And if ever there is any one particular period of the season that is highly indicative of the Barbels' preferences toward feeding nocturnally it is during these colder months.

Without wishing to lead any of you down some misguided path that daytime winter Barbel fishing is entirely futile, any successes during such times tend to fall to the more experienced opportunist who recognises the importance of being able to fish within a moment's notice. This will become more clearly understood as the section unfolds. But we should all remain aware that the importance of our fishing into the winter hours of darkness simply could not be over emphasised.

Although the importance of water temperature and warm south-westerly winds is now extremely well documented, more recent years have witnessed a rising interest towards the belief that certain lunar phases may also play a highly significant role within the Barbels' feeding pattern. An extensive amount of nation-wide data relating to the exact times of many individual Big Barbel captures has now been analysed, and there appears to be evidence that the moon may well have played some part in the majority of them. Whilst I remain open minded with regard to this fascinating subject, I still prefer to err on the side of caution by believing that so many other individual contributory factors also play their role in assisting our good fortune.

WATER TEMPERATURE

Up until recently, the majority of winter Barbel anglers concurred that water temperature was everything when it came to assessing the potential of any one particular winter session. More of us now realise that while our consistent monitoring of the temperature is undoubtedly of crucial importance, the taking of any one singular reading rarely tells us anything.

As their metabolic rate gradually reduces from autumn onwards, the Barbel will enter a varying number of virtually inactive, almost semi-hibernating states, therefore a marked reduction in their feeding patterns and daytime activity will be noticed. As there appears to be many conflicting opinions as to exactly when this process begins, my own records seem to indicate an autumnal water temperature of 12 degrees Celsius would not be too wide of the mark.

Whilst we should perhaps accept that any such measurements may vary from river to river, we must also remain aware that once the first downward spiral of autumn temperatures begin to take hold, there is every likelihood that the resident Barbel population within any venue becomes effected to some degree.

My own experience tells me that the effects of fluctuating temperatures can be understood a little more clearly on a cold water spate river, as this offers us the chance to witness the Barbels' reaction to what I now call the yo-yo effect. When fishing the Derbyshire Dove, for example, it is quite common for a consistent and regular pattern of feeding at 13 to 14 degrees Celsius to become severely disrupted by a sharp fall of only two degrees. Moreover, it's in no way unusual for the Barbel to take a period of at least a week to become acclimatised. This first noticeable drop of the season's water temperature could well be one of the hardest that the species has to contend with, as such a lengthy period of reluctance to indulge in any form of feeding activity would appear to indicate.

These periods of acclimatisation, whilst they may vary in their length, undoubtedly continue throughout the entire duration of autumn and winter, consequently resulting in the species' increasing (though by no means complete) lack of need to feed during the day. As a huge part of this process certainly appears to be brought about by the cooling of the water, it is therefore still widely believed that one major contributory factor in bringing a response to an angler's hook-bait during such a period is any significant rise in temperature. Whilst this popular theory is very often substantiated and well heeded, it also remains in our best interests to note that predominantly nocturnal feeding activity often resumes after only a few days of cooler, but consistent temperature. Providing of course that such a temperature is within the Barbels' metabolic range, i.e. not too cold.

For this example: let us assume that an early winter water temperature of 8 degrees Celsius has recently fallen to 7C and remained consistent for a few days. There is every possibility that the Barbel will have become accustomed to this and be willing to feed – at least, nocturnally. Let us now imagine that the temperature begins another, but more rapid descent (the metabolism of the Barbel will immediately begin to slow) and then settles at 5 degrees C for a few hours. In all probability, the Barbel will now be in temporary shutdown and quite reluctant, even possibly unable, to feed.

Now imagine that an uncharacteristically warm winter's night pushes the water temperature back up slightly to 6C. The theory now being that prospects are equally as good as they were before the drop. Some may argue they are even better as the Barbel will have experienced yet another temporary blip in their metabolism. At the risk of over complicating matters; if we go back one stage; to where the water had settled at 5C; had this remained constant for, say, three days, instead of only a few hours, the Barbel would quite probably have resumed their nocturnal feeding habits. We could then have begun to fish for them appropriately.

I wish it were as simple as this one example indicates. The fact is; however, it isn't – especially when we bring in the widely believed theory that the species enters into its most comatose of conditions when temperatures fall below 4 degrees Celsius. While this theory may well have been proven inconclusive by a number of captures made in much colder conditions than 4C (notably mainly after dark), it would certainly appear that there are far fewer Barbel captured around such a temperature. But then there are far fewer anglers willing to brave the elements to even attempt it.

Another popular belief is that a water temperature of around 6 degrees Celsius makes a good mid-winter benchmark upon which we can often rely. This supposition is partly substantiated by regular captures and could well be used by the relative newcomer as a confidence boosting introductory guideline. However, the more accustomed we become to the winter Barbels' persistence in ensuring that we often question this theory, the more we are likely to become aware that such a benchmark temperature may not exist at all.

Even though we now understand only a little of the complexities involved with fishing throughout these colder months, we should already be aware of the significance of our carrying a thermometer. It very often pays great dividends for the winter specialist to constantly monitor water temperatures, take note of any minor but often significant rises or prolonged periods of stability, and respond to them accordingly.

Whenever possible, temperature readings are far better taken on a daily basis or, at the very least, every other day. It's always extremely helpful if a mate can make it to the river on those occasions that we cannot. We can always return the compliment. A point worth noting, though, is that whenever any two different thermometers are used, even of identical types, there may well be a marked variation between each individual reading. It therefore makes sense to compare them both as soon as possible. Once this is done, we may then accept that a reading of 6 degrees Celsius on our own thermometer could easily be met with a reading of say, 5.5 on our colleague's. It amazes me just how many winter Barbel anglers are unaware of these differences, but they're as common as those variations between weighing scales.

The emphasis of importance now lies within our willingness to keep in consistent touch with our venue: our success will very often depend on it. We should also consider that periods of persistent freezing temperatures are probably bettered spent in the arms of a good woman, man, or doing whatever else may take our fancy. As the fish are unlikely to be very active in these conditions, we really need only take note of when they improve.

After only a few weeks of cool weather experience, providing we have made the necessary effort, we should already begin to see how ridiculously predictable the winter Barbel can be. So much so, that many specialists now begin their season in October and ignore the summer months completely. When we also consider that each individual Big Barbel usually weighs considerably more in winter than it does in summer, their seemingly more predictable cool weather feeding habits should further encourage us to fish the whole winter through.

This in no way implies that we won't get it all wrong from time to time, but it should quickly become apparent how productive a rising water temperature can be. Particularly when brought about by warm south-westerly wind and rain; and the more the better. It will also pay us to note that the period the fish take to acclimatise to any drop in temperature appears to shorten as the winter progresses.

We should soon realise that the more we make use of the darkness the higher percentage of success we will enjoy. And this doesn't mean that we have to fish all night! The bulk of my own winter sessions are now rarely more than two and a half hours long, and that includes the time that it takes me to set up and pack up. Should conditions be ideal, and it's dark by 5.00pm, I arrive at my chosen swim by 4.30pm and I'm walking back to the car by 7.00pm. I'm always prepared for a bite at exactly the moment the sky turns black and my beta-lights begin to glow at their brightest. A bite won't always be forthcoming, but 75% of my winter caught Big Barbel say that it probably will!

Another point worth noting before reading the summery below, is that of past recommendations that we should continue to monitor water temperatures whilst we are fishing. Although this could be arguably necessary in the event that we were to fish sessions of a long duration, it is highly unlikely that we will need to take any reading beyond the beginning of a short, dusk into darkness, session. After all, we are actually taking regular readings to maximise our knowledge of when would be the most appropriate time to fish; that way we should be able to avoid the need to fish long winter sessions. This should also ensure that we maximise our chances of avoiding the symptoms of demoralisation.

KNOWING WHEN TO FISH
(USING ONLY WATER TEMPERATURE AS A GUIDLINE)

This summary example outlines the most important points on water temperature that I feel we must consider, and to simplify things it is based on the assumption that the 4C theory is correct.

Daytime feeding activity becomes less frequent with reducing water temperatures, and the Barbel needs time to acclimatise to any significant drop. For acclimatisation to occur, the water temperature must stabilise to a level of at least 4C in mid winter. The length of time it takes for the fish to adjust to these changes appears to shorten as the winter progresses; i.e. from around 1 week initially, to approximately 3 days in mid winter.

Once the Barbel has adjusted to any stabilised reduction in water temperature, at least brief spells of nocturnal feeding activity will be resumed. The cooler the conditions, the shorter any feeding spell is likely to be. Rising water temperature appears to briefly re-activate daytime feeding activity, the duration of which is likely to be dependent on the significance of any such rise. Warm south-westerly wind and rain is likely to prolong any feeding spell; be it during the day or night.

It really becomes clear when you sit down to write about temperature that it is one of the most difficult areas to convey, undoubtedly because there are far too many variables. I feel, however, that I have touched on the most significant of them; the rest will become apparent once your own winter campaign is under way.

UNDER PRESSURE

After little more than two years of fairly consistent study, I have now adopted the beliefs of the increasing number of specialists who follow the theory that fluctuating air pressures may well play a highly significant role in our prospects. Although they also appear relative to summer, any fluctuations in these warmer months tend to occur less frequently, probably as a direct result of the consistent high pressures that we often associate with this time of year.

Winter, on the other hand, is renowned for bringing with it many irregular patterns of both high and low pressures, and my short but seemingly reliable study seems to indicate that a barometer could be almost an important an instrument to the Barbel angler as the thermometer. Once we become accustomed to the ways in which air pressures appear to influence the Barbels' feeding activity, we will then be in the position to combine any appropriate barometric readings with current water temperatures and note how the prospects of our catching improves.

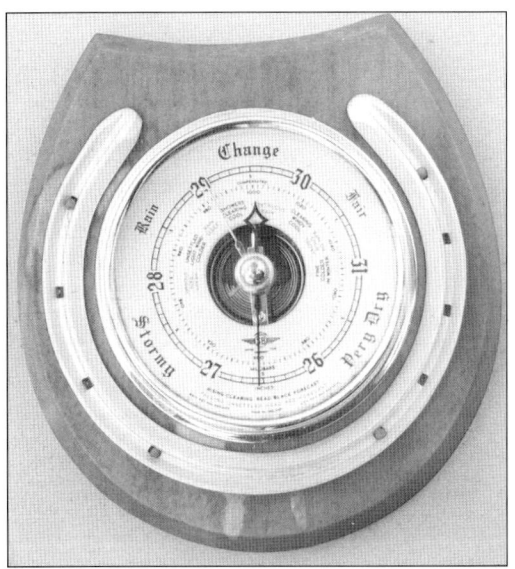

The best example I can give as to how the Barbel may become under pressure to feed is, ironically, in late summer; in a situation that just about every one of us will have encountered. All we need to do is cast our minds back to when we last experienced fishing just before, during and after an unexpected thunderstorm. What is extremely common to this situation is that a prolonged period of high pressure is dramatically disrupted by a rapid and notably large fall.

Also a common occurrence, providing we have Barbel in our swim, is that we often begin to experience bites at a time that coincides with the pressure drop. Even when we haven't had the slightest knock for hours, the moment that the Heaven's open up is likely to be the point we need to grab the rod as it is almost pulled into the river by a hungry Barbel. Moreover, it is likely that the fish will feed avidly until the storm subsides.

It would be easy for those of us who are uneducated towards the possible influences of changing air pressures to assume that the falling rain itself is the feeding trigger, but the theory indicates that this is simply not the case. The key appears more likely to be within the fallen pressure itself or, more accurately in this instance, the speed at which it fell and the shortness of duration for which it stayed. What the sceptics need to consider is that for each example that could be given in which it rained, there is also another where the air pressure will have fallen in similar circumstances in which it didn't rain, but the fish fed throughout the duration of the low pressure.

We don't always need to look at a barometer to be aware that any such changes in atmospheric conditions have occurred, as they can often be felt at the time that we are fishing; the most common of them being a sudden apparent heaviness, humidity, or coolness within our surroundings.

As is often described by followers of the moonrise, moonset theory, it's also common for a drop in air pressure to be briefly accompanied by a sudden breeze that drops to stillness almost as quickly as it appears. All of these individual changes can be attributed to rapidly falling air pressures, and whilst they are far more easily noticeable during the summer months they may well act as a feeding trigger at any time throughout the season.

Sudden and dramatic drops in winter air pressure are easily recognisable when a built up area is within our view and a smoking chimney can be observed. Proving there is very little or no wind, a low pressure is virtually guaranteed to force the smoke to leave the chimney at an acute, almost horizontal, angle; the heavier the pressure drop, the further down the smoke will be pushed. A high pressure, on the other hand, is indicated by the opposite extreme, when the smoke can often be seen to leave the chimney in a direct vertical line towards the sky.

On the strength of the evidence given so far, it would be easy to assume that we should constantly remain on the lookout for low pressure, when, in reality, we are actually looking for a change in either direction. It just happens that considerably infrequent high to low pressure change is more conducive to the summer months. In autumn and winter, though, the subject becomes rather more open and interestingly more predictable, simply as a direct result of the weather's reluctance to favour any one particular extreme; for no sooner have we settled into a period of low pressure than along comes a high, and visa-versa.

It appears our ideal is an interruption in any prolonged weather pattern that has remained constant for a period in which air pressures have remained consistently rising, falling, or steady for a minimum of three consecutive days. Go on read that again! It's also important that the water temperature is within the Barbels' metabolic range and has remained so for at least the same period.

For this example: let us imagine that we are in the month of December and have a water temperature of 5C and a low pressure, both of which have remained stable for a period of three days. Having kept an eye on the barometer on a daily basis, we then observe that on the fourth day there is a considerable upturn in air pressure. This is our cue to fish, just as it would have been had the pressures been reversed. We should note that the closer we fish to the change, the higher our prospects often appear to be.

Something that also appears to improve our prospects even further is when a pressure change coincides with a rising water temperature. The most commonly recognisable example being of those instances where the now famous warm south-westerly wind and rain suddenly interrupt a sustained period of cool high pressure.

These are very often red-letter days for many a winter Barbel angler, and should be noted by us all as must fish days. The barometer can be used to give us our moment's notice, as the falling pressure is often indicated hours before the rain arrives. Those who are fortunate enough to begin fishing before the downpour will be in the position to note that the Barbel are quite likely to have already begun to feed.

When the rain does eventually arrive, this is what gives us our rising water temperature and sustains the feeding spell. I truly believe that in this instance, it really is as simple as that.

Chris Newbold with a Dove 10.00 captured at the time of a pressure drop.

After only a relatively short study, I already suspect that certain particular fluctuations are more likely to interrupt the Barbels' otherwise predominantly winter preference to feed nocturnally by temporarily re-inducing daytime activity. Whilst such activity can be readily witnessed in the situation given in the above example, it appears the Barbel are just as likely to feed (if only briefly) during the day no matter in what direction any change occurs. But, it does appear important that any such change should be both rapid and vast, and that water temperature is at least stable.

For this example: let us imagine that we are again in the month of December. We have a water temperature of 5C that has remained stable for a minimum of three consecutive days and a high pressure that has been around for 1 week. The Barbel in this instance would be more inclined to feed nocturnally and, consequently, we are obviously better to fish only from dusk into darkness.

Now imagine that day four brings a dramatic fall in air pressure, but brings with it no sign of rain or water temperature change. Providing that we can again begin our session as closely to the change as possible, we are likely to witness at least a short period of daytime feeding activity. It's also likely that any nocturnal feeding spell, which coincides with such a change, may well be of a longer duration than if the pressure had remained constant.

It shouldn't take much for us to now imagine the potential of what may happen in those situations where the moon may be rising or setting in its most appropriate cycle; and a warm south westerly wind with a falling air pressure and a rising water temperature occurs. Just the thought of it makes me want to go fishing: the only problem is that it's $-5C$ outside at the time I'm writing this. I think I'll stay where it's warm.

BEWARE THE CRYSTAL BALL

When we begin to substantiate any theory with what appears to be factual evidence, we immediately open ourselves up to the dangers of becoming obsessed by it. Not only do we repeatedly scour through our own past facts and figures, we then compare the findings with those of others, and before we know it are attempting to use the accumulated data as a kind of instrument for predicting the future.

As far as Barbel feeding patterns are concerned, we are certainly beginning to understand these a little further, but it's important that we don't rely entirely on the results of our past successes. It's all well and good to use any half substantiated theory as an indicative guide to our future prospects, but we should always account for those instances in which the Barbel will prove our predictions inconclusive.

It matters not upon which theory our prediction is based, for we do ourselves no favours at all by allowing our fishing to become totally governed by either of them. We would then be merely robbing ourselves of potentially productive opportunities to fish between our predicted times. As for maximising our chances, there will never be any substitute for sitting on the bank with a bait in the water. Consequently, our chances become greatly improved when our instincts are placed along side any theory.

BAIT SIZE AND QUANTITY

An important aspect of winter fishing that is often overlooked is the size of bait we choose to use. Persistently cool temperatures often indicate that we need to reduce our bait size and therefore, as the big bait method becomes less effective, our potential options for fishing selectively are proportionately reduced.

Not only do Barbel need to feed less frequently in these temperatures, they also appear likely to require less food on the occasions they do eat. My own findings appear to indicate that temperatures below 7 degrees Celsius may need to be particularly noted. This is the point at which I now begin to make changes, especially in the event that the temperature has recently fallen. Instead of cutting 300gm can of meat into six, I then begin cutting it into nine pieces, as these appear more likely to be accepted. When using meat-baits of this size I much prefer to use flavoured hook-baits only; and only rarely introduce any free offerings into the swim before leaving.

As previously mentioned, flavoured, dead maggots come into their own at this time of year. When using these, I prefer to place no more than two droppers full of previously frozen ones into the swim prior to introducing a hook-bait. Gassed maggots are always used on the hook. Another option is to place the gassed maggot rig along with the previously frozen ones into a PVA bag, tie it, and place it in the desired spot. At night, this rarely needs to be more than a rod length out! In the event that water temperatures again begin to rise above 7C, bait size is increased accordingly.

GRID FISHING
(WINTER LOCATION)

As already stated in location, in many instances a highly productive summer snag-swim will often produce throughout the entire duration of autumn and winter, particularly when such a swim is normally of a moderate low-water pace and present on a small to medium sized river. However, while the bulk of our Big Barbel swim location is always better done before the onset of winter, there will always remain those instances throughout the colder months in which we are left with very little choice other than to search out new potential winter hotspots. This may be as a direct result of fluctuating water levels on our favourite stretch of water, or in the instances that we are familiarising ourselves with a new venue. But, for whatever the reasons we may need to seek out new winter swims, it's highly likely that most of our searching will need to be done blindly.

On big rivers such as the Trent, it's common for long stretches of water to be almost devoid of the species altogether. While this situation is often brought about by the Barbels' need to seek out well oxygenated water during summer (when many Big fish are found close to shallow rapids and below weir-pools), it becomes extremely important that we find those areas into which these specimens migrate as the season progresses.

Many specialists who feel more at home on smaller venues shudder at the merest thought of attempting to fish a river the size of the Trent, when they really shouldn't be so put off by it. At the risk of sounding blatantly obvious, all they really need to consider is that a big river is nothing more than a larger version of a smaller river. And that where there may be a Big Barbel swim every 300 yards on a smaller venue, they may need to expand this to, say, half a mile on a much larger one.

A method that works exceedingly well when used to locate Big Barbel in either familiar or rather more unfamiliar territory, whether our chosen venue is large or small, is grid fishing. The only considerable variations to be accounted for when fishing a large venue as opposed to a smaller one, is that more weight is likely to be needed to hold down the terminal rig, and that casting distance will occasionally need to be increased.

To make full use of the method, we need to consider the theory that, during winter, the Barbel is often unlikely to move very far from its position of rest to intercept a bait, particularly during the day. It is widely believed that during these most difficult of conditions, for a bite to become even remotely possible, a hook-bait must be presented to within inches of the Barbels' snout. It therefore makes sense that to locate them during such times, we will need to cover the area of any potential swim as comprehensively as possible. This becomes a little easier when we begin fishing in a pre-determined and systematic fashion by mapping out our plan of attack.

The idea behind the grid method is that we divide each swim into sections. This division should be done both across the width and down the length of the swim. When fishing larger swims on big rivers, we may need to consider dividing these into a number of mini-sections to assist us in achieving a more comprehensive coverage. Although the number and size of each individual section will be dependent on the entire area of any one particular swim, three divisions across and three down the length will make a good explanatory example. As our aim is then to use each divisional point as a reference for casting, the plan is best drawn on a piece of paper.

The easiest way to divide the length of our swim is to use both near and far bank fixtures as our guidelines – or markers if you prefer. These can be anything ranging from trees and/or specific branches that hang from them, to fence posts, rocks, or certain positions among dying reed beds, etc, etc…

Division of the river's width, on the other hand, is slightly more difficult for us to measure and will be based a little more on our accuracy of judgement. However, the fact that we are outlining our plan on paper makes this more difficult task a little easier to overcome. All we really need to do is familiarise ourselves with what we believe to be the point of mid-river.

On a particularly wide river, providing that we can reach it, we could choose to make the middle the furthest point to which we cast. On a smaller river, we will undoubtedly have the option to cast further if we so choose. Depending upon the characteristics of the swim, all we need to decide is whether or not we believe that the fish may be lying past the halfway point before making our plan.

For this example: let us imagine that we are to fish a small river swim that offers us a maximum potential feeding area of 20 metres width by 30 metres in length. We have decided to fish beyond the halfway point, which in this case is 20 metres from the bank. As the swim is actually 40 metres wide, our decision is based on the assumption that we regard the first 10-metre span of water immediately in front of us, and the final 30 to 40 metres as likely to be non-productive. We then need to draw three parallel lines that cover the entire length and follow the shape of the potential feeding area. In this instance, the first will be drawn 10 metres from the bank, the second at 20 metres (which marks the middle) and the third at 30 metres from our bank.

By using whichever markers we have chosen to assist us, all that we need to do then is to draw the same number of parallel lines going straight across from our bank to the opposite. With our map (grid) now complete, we will now see that we have nine points where the lines cross over. These are the points into which we should cast our hook-bait, and we really only need leave this in position for around 10 minutes before retrieving and casting to the next spot. When using this method, my own preference is to fish the most downstream points first; usually beginning at the furthest point away from me and finishing at the nearest. The reason for this is not only because I believe that starting here is less likely to spook any fish that may well be sitting upstream, but also because, for some strange reason, these positions tend to produce fish more rapidly. Maybe it's just another one of those inexplicable things!

It's worth our while to consider that the weight necessary to hold bottom in the stronger currents of the swim is likely to be more than is needed in the calmer water. It is therefore in our best interests to employ a quick-change rig so that we can make any appropriate adjustments. We aren't trying to achieve so much of a critical balance here, as this would take too long and would be likely to cause a little too much swim disturbance. Nevertheless, we do need to ensure that we keep the rig as sensitive and resistance-free as possible. After all, with bites likely to be very hard to come by, we certainly don't want the fish to refuse the bait through poor presentation. Where circumstances allow, i.e. it's not too cold to the fingers, touch legering is our best method of bite detection.

Although this method is highly suited to our using flavoured single hook-baits only; it occasionally pays us to deposit one dropper load of hemp at the head of each particular run of sections: we could also consider hemp bombs as an option.

A 10.14 captured on the second cast of a grid session

FISHING IN THE DARK

As we really have little choice in becoming at least temporary night-owls, we will need to make things as easy for ourselves as possible. There is seldom a happy medium struck between anglers regarding night fishing; it seems either we love it or we hate it.

The dividing line between this preference or non-preference is often down to little more than how warm and comfortable we feel whilst fishing. Perhaps if we are truly honest with ourselves, we could all look back at the times we have half frozen to death and been drenched in the process. Even just as likely, we may recall fumbling around without adequate lighting and/or straining our eyes to near blindness trying to see that dying starlight perched at the tip of our rod. The things we do to catch Barbel!

We make things far easier for ourselves when we become fully prepared. I hope that this little guide helps.

1. SIGHT. For general sight such as unhooking fish, setting up the camera, etc.
Head torch. Small waterproof pocket torch. Spare batteries. Spare bulbs.
2. BITE INDICATION. Fit two beta-light attachments in the positions indicated.
Beta-light x two. Minimum 600 power. Middy offers good value.

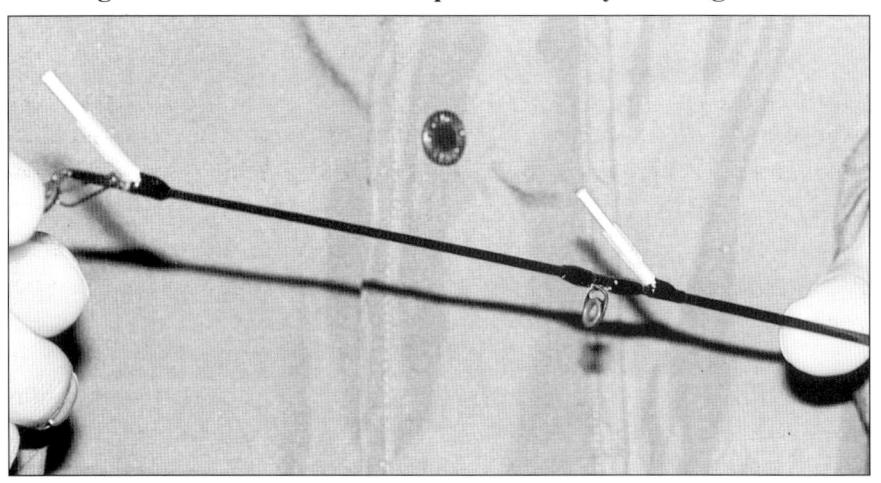

3. CLOTHING. It is essential that we remain warm and dry throughout each session.
One-piece Thermal suit. Thermal boots. (Derri- boots) Thermal socks.
4. TACKLE. To assist us in keeping warm, we must shelter from wind and rain.
Umbrella.

Although my suggested Brand names may be kept optional, I would certainly recommend that all of these items we make compulsory.

For further useful information on winter tactics, I advise that reference be made to the following book. **Quest for Barbel. Edition 1 or 2: by Trefor West and Tony Miles.**

CHAPTER 5

REPRODUCTION
PHOTOGRAPHING FISH
CONCLUSION
BIG BARBEL HANDLING CODE
USEFUL ADDRESSES

REPRODUCTION

Even though there will always be those instances of unnatural exception, it remains a virtual certainty that any Barbel we catch in excess of seven pounds will be female. Therefore, it would appear in this instance that Big is most definitely beautiful; and as the main topic of the book is centred on big, beautiful females, I couldn't resist the temptation to include a section on sex and reproduction. With a slight difference, of course!

I know most of us have a good old moan about the rising prices of national fishing rod licences, and we probably find it easy to imagine some old Environment Agency fat cats running big, expensive motors and generally living a life of luxury. But how often do we stop to consider where the proportionate costs of our investment actually end up being spent? If I were to tell you that a percentage of our fee went towards a kind of artificial insemination and temporary fostering program, would you believe me? Probably not. But the fact is – it's true. For you see, an extremely high number of Barbel and other species of coarse fish are nurtured through The Environment Agency's breeding programme which is based at Calverton Fish

Farm, a few miles Northeast of Nottingham.

This highly professional set-up is a credit to the guys who run it; and as far as Barbel fostering goes, the futures of millions of our favourite species simply could not be in safer hands. Manned 24 hours per day, this 16-acre site accommodates a laboratory, warm water hatchery, nurseries and no less than 35 stock ponds. There are five full time members of staff at Calverton – Farm Manager, Alan Henshaw; plus his team of, Nick Eyre, Ian Rockley, Neil Lincoln, and Kevin Fanthorpe. All are keen anglers themselves, and justifiably proud of what they have achieved on the farm.

The Barbel is the only member of the carp family (cyprinid species) to produce non-sticky spawn. A relatively small female Barbel of only 5 pounds will produce 5,000 to 10,000 yellow coloured eggs (see colour section). In their natural river environment, the eggs are laid amongst the gravel, and in many instances only a small (but arguably naturally balanced) minority of the fry (tiny barbel) that emerge from them would go on to reach maturity. The ideal, predatory and disease-free conditions at Calverton however ensure that most will thrive; and with such an assurance that fish of every species are infection-free comes an extremely high demand.

Calverton's massive stocking programme – the biggest of its kind in the United Kingdom – is already responsible for adding a new lease of life to previously dying angling rivers such as the Staffordshire Tame, and Yorkshire's Don and Rother. Three quarters of the Barbel produced at Calverton are used to replenish stocks lost by pollution, and to re-populate formerly fishless rivers completely free of charge. The rest are sold on to angling clubs to ensure that running costs of the farm are covered.

For Barbel spawning activity to begin, the water temperature must remain constantly between 16 and 18 degrees Celsius for two to three days, and usually occurs within the first two weeks of May. (And who says Barbel don't spawn during the closed season?) The fresh, healthy brood fish that Calverton use are selected mainly from the Trent, and to avoid narrowing the gene pool, these are borrowed from different locations every year. By keeping a close eye on the long-range weather forecast, the lads are able to time their brood-fish collecting run to perfection. Once permission has been granted from the appropriate angling club, around 20 male and 20 female Barbel, each weighing between three and seven pounds will then be electrofished from the river. After being transported back to the farm, they are then held in quarantine tanks and given a thorough health check. Although these brood fish will be held captive for a maximum of only 48 hours, an interesting point to note is that should they be kept indefinitely, just by controlling the amount of light and making the appropriate adjustments in temperature, spawning could be encouraged to occur every 21 days.

Barbel transportation is safe, comfortable and secure!

The selected females may produce over 180,000 fry, around 60,000 of which are selected to grow on for up to two years to reach a target weight of around 8 ounces. The other 120,000 are released back into the wild. A real big problem originally faced by fishery staff was inducing the females to spawn once removed from their natural environment. This is overcome by the use of a powerful hormone that is extracted from the pituitary glands contained in the brains of dead carp; the meat of which is farmed for human consumption in Rumania and the Czech Republic. Although the hormone itself is expensive, at around £200 per gram, there is plenty to ensure that millions of new fish are created. No Carp are killed purposely to extract the gland for, as a by-product, this would normally end up as animal fodder.

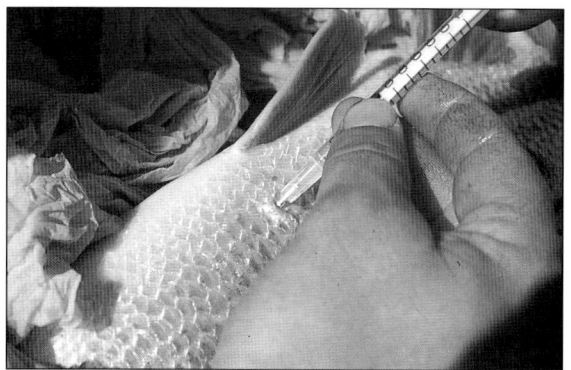

Once the hormone has been ground down, it is then injected into each female (above left) to induce her to spawn.

Left. Female vent primed and ready for egg laying.

Left. Female is stripped of eggs.

The female eggs and male milt are then stripped by hand and thoroughly mixed for fertilisation.

Even in these days of modern technology, this still has to be done with a swan or goose feather! The eggs are then stored at the perfect temperature for incubation and will usually hatch within seven days.

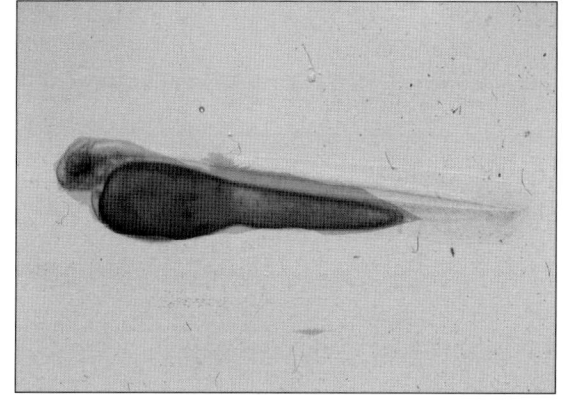

Once hatched, the larvae are then fed on tiny invertebrates until their stomachs are developed enough for them to be weaned onto high protein pellets.

Left. One-day-old barbel larva, with large yolk sack visible.

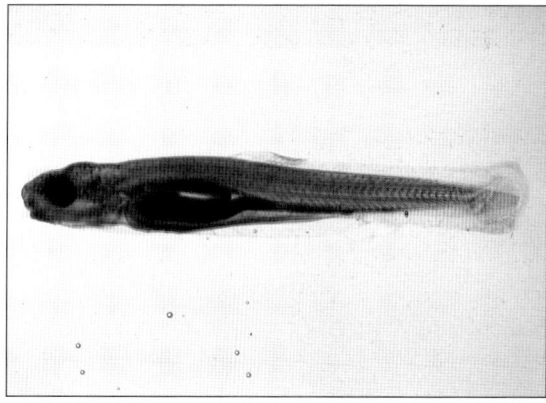

Left. Eleven days after hatching with swimbladder and food gut visible.

By controlling the amount of heat and light, the fry are literally fooled into believing that it's summer the whole year round, and therefore can be induced to gain weight quite rapidly. Once they become of an appropriate length, the still relatively small Barbel are then transferred to a large, fully enclosed growing pond, the richly coloured water of which is packed with natural food (zooplankton). The fish grow from five inches during the first 12 months, to between nine and ten inches at the end of the second year. They are then ready for release into whichever water requires them.

The first 12 months of their lives is spent under cover.

This one's in its second year and looks a little more like the real thing.

Said Alan: *"It's obvious the whole staff believe in the work they do, and are committed to improving the quality of our water life. The work that we carry out here is groundbreaking stuff, and to be part of that gives you a real buzz!"*

My very special thanks go to Alan and his team, and to Upper Trent Fisheries Scientist, Tim Jacklin, for granting me this visit.

PHOTOGRAPHING FISH

Many of us like to keep at least one photographic momento of our better captures, but how often do we end up disappointed with the results of our efforts? For lots of specialist anglers photography can be a nightmare, particularly whilst attempting to take self-portraits when we are lacking in the experience needed to do so, adequately. Also, because having someone else take our photos can be equally disappointing; it remains in our own best interests to familiarise ourselves with the joys of that wonderful little invention, the self-timer. I hope this segment will provide enough useful tips to further ensure that our heads, vital limbs, and the entire fish, are all included in the photo. Moreover, that our self-portraits remain centred, fully framed and crisply in focus.

These days, there is very little need to pay over the odds for a point and shoot, fully automatic, 35mm compact camera. Providing the automatic focusing mechanism is infrared or similar, and 'is not' of the fixed focal (and usually cheaper) type, we should be fine. We should ensure our choice has a tripod socket, built in flash, and at least a 10-second self-timer. Wherever possible, I would also advise that we choose a model with a built-in wide-angle lens of 28 or 30 mm. This is not crucial, but it will offer a bigger margin for error than the slightly larger 35mm. Another advantage in having this facility is that the camera can be held a little closer to the subject, and so is particularly useful for flash photography in total darkness.

We aren't likely to be spoilt for choice when looking for compact, wide-zoom cameras, as there aren't that many about. At the time of writing, I have an Argos book with me and there appears to be one that may be suitable. This is a Nikon 70W 28 – 70 Zoom at £79.00. Catalogue number 561/7254. This appears good value and gives us the option to increase the focal length should we wish to do so. Other brands that I believe to market them include Olympus and Samsung. Reasonably priced cameras that begin at 35mm are much easier to find and may come a little cheaper. Check out the Konica Z-UP 70VP. 35 – 70 Zoom at £59.99. Number 561/5452 and the Vivitar Mega 100S at £54.99. Number 561/7704. Please check with Argos for current availability!

The potential quality of photographs from any of the above cameras is more than adequate for our requirements, and as we will be using fully automatic exposure – providing our model is working correctly – the majority of problems we are likely to encounter will be pretty much down to ourselves.

Common problems associated with self-timer photography usually range from 1: subject cut-off – mainly off centre 2: subject too far away, hence too small 3: subject out of focus 4: subject too dark, either day or night. Many of us I'm sure have been victims of all of these at some point or other, and more times than we may care to admit have probably been stung for a tenner's worth of film and prints that were just about fit for the rubbish bin. Photography is not cheap, and so we need to get it right.

Problem 1. Cut-off.
To rectify this most common of problems we must first learn to use the viewfinder instead of attempting to position ourselves correctly in relation to the lens. It's surprising just how many anglers try this. But it is most definitely not surprising how many get it wrong!

Every brand new camera comes complete with a handbook, and although most will outline what we will see through the viewfinder, it's highly unlikely that we will be advised of how to photograph our Barbel. An essential point to remember for quality photos is that we must fill the frame. Cut-off occurs mainly because the subject is off centre, most commonly resulting from our standing too far to one side. 'If only I'd moved the fish a bit that way?' probably sounds familiar. I've had a good few of these myself in the past, but as you can see by the brilliant example of how NOT to do it (supplied by a friend who wishes to remain anonymous); self-timed photography can prove to be a bit of a handful. On the other hand, is it 'waderful?'

When looking through a modern viewfinder to frame our subject, we should see something close to the example given below.

PHOTOGRAPHY.135

The centre is marked by an inner square and represents our guide for the auto-focus mechanism. The outer square, or angles, we can use to keep the subject centrally within the frame. It is incorrect for us to assume this outer square represents the outside edge at which our final print will be cut, as we would then risk the subject appearing too far away.

As we cannot frame ourselves standing in front of the camera whilst looking through the viewfinder, we need the guidance of something in the background that we can then preferably sit or crouch against when taking our shot. Parts of our umbrella and/or the top of the backrest on our chair are particularly useful in the dark. All we need do is to shine our torch on any relevant points of focus while looking through the viewfinder. Although we can make use of virtually anything that gives us a perspective of width and depth of photo, parts of bushes, trees, fences, clumps of nettles or reed-beds, etc, can all be useful during the day.

What the finished photograph should look like.

The examples given here are shot at 28mm. Although we will need to check in our own camera's handbook, most infra-red auto-focus systems allow us a focal range from as close as 0.45m (1.48ft) to infinity. If we were to stand perfectly centred within the system's minimal optical range of 1.48ft, we would remain sharply in focus but would experience extreme cut-off. However, just over double at 1.1m (3.72ft approx.) would be our ideal. Although this may still appear a little on the close side, it surprisingly offers us a margin for error, which allows for approximately half an inch either side of a standard 6in x 4in print.

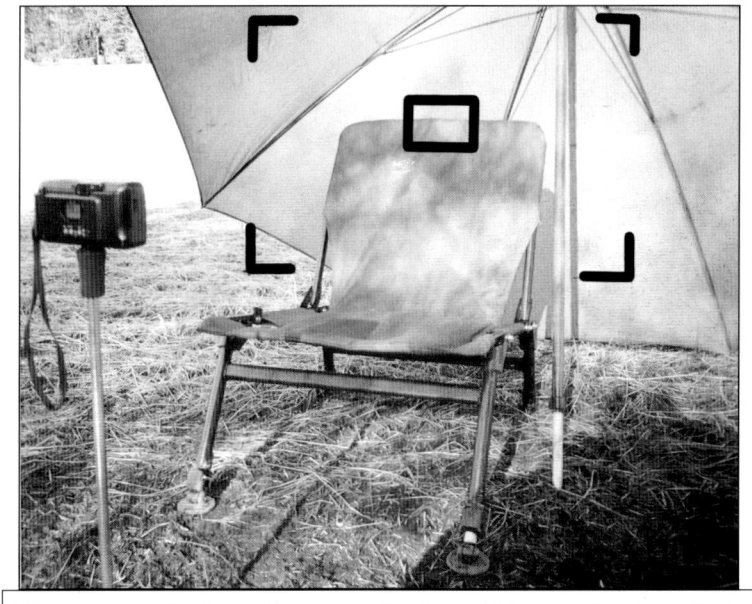

This photo again shows focus area for those of us no taller than 5'10.

Having the camera this close allows us easy frontal access to the shutter release button. As our aim is to set the self-timer whilst framing the shot from behind, the fact that we then activate the trip-switch from the front, by leaning only slightly forward, gives us the full 10 seconds in which to take up our position with the fish. However, as our main priority is the Barbel's welfare, we must ensure that the fish is retained in the water until our equipment is fully positioned and the photo ready for taking. (I.e. just before we are ready to activate the self-timer.) The Barbel can then be carefully cradled in our lap when sitting, or resting within easy reach by our side when crouching, as we press the shutter release button. We then have 10 seconds to position the fish, pose and say cheese.

This 11.3 is the ideal example.

As with photographing them, holding our Barbel appropriately comes naturally with practice. Taking extra care to position our hands, as far around the back of the fish as possible, we must then ensure that the side we want to photograph is held squarely to the lens and is level with our chest. This is always made far easier when we are also centrally behind it. When sitting in my chair or crouching next to, say, a clump of nettles, I sit the camera on top of a 3ft bankstick via a home-made adapter, which I screw into the tripod socket located at the bottom of the camera. This is far more convenient than carrying a tripod around. Although adapters are easily made (see photo), they can also be purchased in specialist tackle shops. By effectively curing problem 1, we have also rectified numbers 2 and 3.

Problem 4. Too dark.

Pointing the camera in the direction of bright sunshine will virtually guarantee that our daytime photography turns out too dark. Even when our particular model is fitted with a back light correction facility, we will avoid disappointment more readily by keeping the sun behind us. I appreciate this is a very fundamental rule, but it is often forgotten in the excitement of the moment.

Taking pictures in the dark is our most important area for concern, and providing that we stay within the focal length already described, we need only consider film speed. For lens settings from 28mm to 52mm (well within our range), ISO 200 is completely acceptable for both day and night photography. However, should the zoom of our camera extend beyond 52mm, the manufacturer is likely to recommend ISO 400, as this will ensure adequate performance throughout the entire focal range.

These are my particular favourites. Although the Fuji DL 500 wide is now six years old, they do occasionally appear in the second hand shops for around £25. If you are fortunate enough to come across one then I recommend you buy it. There may be a few Samsung 290W's about though. Well worth checking out! The electrical tape wrapped around the top of the bank stick creates a snug fit over my adapter which is made up with a piece of duplon, a plastic washer and a small bolt with the appropriate thread for the housing on the underside of the camera. This is shown more clearly below.

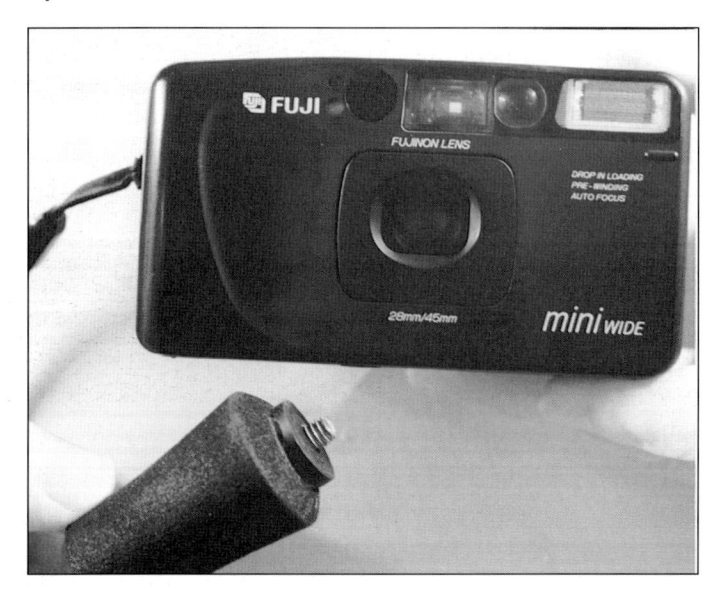

35-mm film can also be expensive, but a particular mid-priced brand that I would most certainly recommend is, Agfa. I very often get three films for less than a fiver and both quality and performance are excellent. A point worth noting is that our photos may appear dark and/or off centre as a direct result of bad printing. In any event that we are disappointed with the results, it always pays to check the negatives. Providing a detailed outline of the subject appears on these, then there is no logical reason why it should not be on the print. If we suspect the printer is at fault then we are perfectly within our rights to ask for a re-print!

In the interests of fish welfare, we should refrain from keeping them out of the water for longer than is necessary. One photograph of each side of the Barbel is really all we need. By using the self-timer in the way described here, the fish needs only be out of the water for a maximum of one and a half minutes!

10lb 7oz.

CONCLUSION

As I began to write this book, it soon became clear that I had so much to cover in each section yet so little amount of space to cover it with. Consequently, as much as I have thoroughly enjoyed writing it, I can't help but feel slightly unfulfilled as I could only touch on certain areas, many of which could easily have been the subjects of at least an entire chapter. (I can already feel a sequel coming on!)

The very essence of the book was always to offer something a little different; something that not only questions some of the traditions within our particular branch of the sport, but I hope offers effective alternatives. As both a first time author and non-conformist, I have tried to strike a balance between tradition and modern technological progression, and to show that there still remains plenty of room between the two. Whether I have been successful is for each and every reader to decide.

For now, I would like to thank you for taking the time to read it, and can only hope that at least part of the book has a positive effect on your fishing.

I will now leave you with this final thought.

'If it ain't broke, don't fix it!' This is a popular phrase often uttered by the specialist Barbel angler who truly believes he is using some ultimate rig or tactic. It's easy to see why this happens, for if he has found a really efficient method he can become extremely set in his ways and very reluctant to try anything new.

To a certain extent I can understand this fixed mentality, but in stark contrast must admit to being the experimental type who is always willing to try something a little different. Anyone who does this will be aware that new ideas often result in blank sessions, but when they are successful, a great sense of achievement is obtained.

Often, all that is required to refine any method or rig is a small tweak here or there, and you only need to look at the many variations of the hair-rig which have come about since its disclosure to understand what I am saying. For me, the endless pursuit of the most efficient bait, rig or method, is part of the reason that I am a Barbel angler.

I believe that to catch Big Barbel consistently we must remain flexible, extremely patient and stealthy, and be willing to mix some of our old ideas with the new. But, no matter how effective any particular method may seem, we must never forget the importance of luck. Without that the bite doesn't come, and 'if there ain't no bite, there ain't no fish!' All we can do is try to sway the luck in our favour by being as attentive as possible in the way we present the bait and who knows; the more we practice this the luckier we may become!

BIG BARBEL HANDLING CODE

Always use at least the tackle strength outlined in this book. Ensure your objective is always to land the Barbel as quickly as possible to ensure minimum distress and exhaustion to the fish. In case of a prolonged battle (particularly in warm water and only where sufficient depth and flow of water allow), adopt the habit of allowing the fish to rest in the landing net for a minimum of 60 seconds before initial removal from the water. Deliberately prolonging a fight causes unnecessary distress to the fish and dramatically increases our chances of losing it.

1. **Take note that line does not last forever.** Examine and test it frequently. If in the slightest doubt then change it. Always begin a new session with a new hook-link. This comes far more naturally when we dismantle rigs and rods at the end of each session and reassemble at the onset of each new one. Leaving line through the rings of a rod that is merely kept in a quiver/rod-bag for days on end is a bad habit that could easily cost you the fish of a lifetime.
2. **Never attempt to land a fish by beaching it.** Use only a large knot-less landing net. When possible unhook the fish in the landing net while still in the water. If this isn't an option, while the fish is still in the net, place onto an unhooking mat – never on bare gravel or stones, etc. Wet your hands before handling the fish.
3. **Remove hooks with good quality forceps.** If necessary cut the line and thread the hook out point first. Examine the mouth for other hooks and carefully remove these also.

4. **Treat mouth sores and wounds with antiseptic creams and/or solutions** such as Kryston Clinic. Dry wounds with a clean towel before applying solution with a cotton bud.
5. **Do not retain Barbel without good reason!** If no photo or weighing is required, return the fish immediately. In the event that a photo is required, refer to the relevant section of this book! Always transfer the Barbel to the required place in the safety of the landing net.
6. **Return the fish in the landing net and allow it to fully recover its strength.** During this period of recovery, hold the head facing upstream in a flow of clean water. Watch for steady working of the gills and the ability of the fish to maintain its balance. Release only when it's obvious that the Barbel can swim powerfully back into the main river.
7. **If an exceptional fish is to be retained,** it should be for the shortest duration possible. Carp type sacks must be used with great caution. Never retain Barbel in keep-nets; they cause damage and stress! Keep-sacks require areas of reasonable depth and flow and should be soaked in water before placing the Barbel within them. Be certain that the sack can be tethered securely.
8. **Ensure that the fish can lie in the sack with its head upstream,** in an upright position and with gills moving freely. Ensure that the Barbel is not curled or twisted in the sack. Inspect it regularly, but with minimum disturbance.

This is in part a summarised version of the Barbel Society Handling code with a few of my own unofficial suggestions.

USEFUL ADDRESSES

SHIMANO UK LTD
LAKESIDE TECHNOLOGY PARK
PHOENIX WAY
LLANSAMLET
SWANSEA
SA7 9EH

BARBEL CATCHERS CLUB
STEVE CHELL
2 BARELEY ROAD
IPSTONES
STOKE ON TRENT
STAFFS
ST10 7QF

THE BARBEL SOCIETY
MEMBERSHIP SECRETARY
JOHN FOUND
158 DOUGLAS ROAD
TOLWORTH
SURBITON
SURREY
KT6 7SE

HARRISON ADVANCED RODS
201 SUMMERS ROAD
BRUNSWICK BUSINESS PARK
LIVERPOOL
L3 4BL
TELE 0151 7095981

ANGLING TIMES
BUSHFIELD HOUSE
ORTON CENTRE
PETERBOROUGH
PE2 5UW
TELE 01733 232600

ANGLERS MAIL
KINGS REACH TOWER
STAMFORD STREET
LONDON
SE19 9LS
TELE 0207 261-5980

KRYSTON PRODUCTS
BOLTON ENTERPRISE CENTRE
WASHINGTON CENTRE
BOLTON
BL3 5EY

DRENNAN INTERNATIONAL
BOCARDO COURT
TEMPLE ROAD
OXFORD
OX4 2EX

A.C.A
SHALFORD DAIRY
ALDERMASTON
READING
BERKS
RG7 4NB

TACKLE SHOPS

ANGLING CENTRE DERBY
27-33 NIGHTINGALE ROAD
DERBY
DE24 8BG
TELE 01332 380605

WALKERS OF TROWEL
NOTTINGHAM ROAD
TROWEL
NOTTINGHAM
NG9 3PA
TELE 0115 9440898

HINDERS FISHING SUPERSTORE
MANOR GARDEN CENTRE
CHENEY MANOR
SWINDON
SN2 2QJ
TELE 01793 333900

BENNETTS OF SHEFFIELD LTD
STANLEY STREET
SHEFFIELD
SOUTH YORKSHIRE
S3 8JP
TELE 0114 2756 756

TREV'S OF WILMSLOW
16 ALTRINCHAM ROAD
WILMSLOW
CHESHIRE
SK9 5ND
TELE 01625 528831

W. M A. C.
UNIT 8
BILLS STREET
DARLASTON
WEST MIDLANDS
WS10 8XB
TELE 0121 5263696

ALFRETON ANGLING CENTRE
11 PARK STREET
ALFRETON
DERBYSHIRE
TELE 01773 832611

ROD AND LINE TACKLE
17 NOTTINGHAM ROAD
RIPLEY
DERBYSHIRE
TELE 01773 749545

TACKLE BOX
323 SOMERCOTES HILL
SOMERCOTES
LEABROKES
DERBYSHIRE
TELE 01773 602985

ANGLERS CORNER
344 OSMASTON ROAD
DERBY
01332 343870

BAITS AND TACKLE ACCESSORIES

ARCHIE BRADDOCKS BAITS
1 WILMOT STREET
LONG EATON
NOTTINGHAMSHIRE
NG10 3GX
TELE 0115 972 6886

SEER PRODUCTS
BOX 88
BROMYARD
HEREFORDSHIRE
HR7 4JS
TELE 01885 490703

DOUBLE T
15 QUEENSWAY TRADING EST
LEAMINGTON SPA
CV31 3LZ
TELE 01926 831161/881627

JOHN BAKER BAITS
(TECHNICAL ADVICE)
(BUSINESS HOURS PLEASE)
TELE 0118 9404837

BARBEL ANGLING TUITION

Although many other specialist anglers and I believe that static bait legering is the most consistently effective way to capture Big Barbel, there are many interesting and varied methods in which to catch the species in general. For those anglers who feel they would like to expand their existing knowledge; learn the art of watercraft; how to present moving baits, and much more, then a day out with either of these two unique anglers may be just up your street.

RAY WALTON
E-MAIL: ray-waltonattalk21.com.
TELE MOBILE. 07751 572419

TREFOR WEST
TELE 02476 454181